TESTIMONIALS

How I maintain the Presence Of God in this *Hectic World.*

Mr. Jaafri is a sincere man seeking to ever improve his relationship with his God. In his book he shares openly and genuinely about how he goes about that and I believe readers will find great value in knowing and experimenting with the techniques he describes that have produced such exceptional results for him.

—**LB**, MSIA MINSTER, Los Angeles, CA

Mushtaq Jaafri's **How to Maintain the Presence of God in this Hectic World** *is a testament to the true meaning of our existence, our being and our relationship with our creator. It's proof that God speaks to us and we speak to him. A relationship with God is the only way to peace and salvation in a world that can sometimes be overwhelming. Mushtaq says I love you God—but, you know that. I believe God says to us, I love you—but, you know that.*

—**Buddy Dow**, Publishing Consultant

Mushtaq Jaafri has done it again with his latest book, **HOW TO MAINTAIN THE PRESENCE OF GOD IN THIS HECTIC WORLD**. *Learn how to connect yourself to the eternal being and live the life you have always dreamed of. Follow a step by step method that is easy to understand and contains many interesting stories to enhance your existence today.*

—**Al Galasso**, Editor, Book Dealers World

HOW TO MAINTAIN THE PRESENCE OF GOD IN THIS HECTIC WORLD

How I Remain in the Presence of God Daily?

Rev. Dr. Mushtaq Jaafri

BALBOA.
PRESS
A DIVISION OF HAY HOUSE

Balboa Press books may be ordered through booksellers or by contacting:

Balboa Press
A Division of Hay House
1663 Liberty Drive
Bloomington, IN 47403
www.balboapress.com
1 (877) 407-4847

Because of the dynamic nature of the Internet, any web addresses or links contained in this book may have changed since publication and may no longer be valid. The views expressed in this work are solely those of the author and do not necessarily reflect the views of the publisher, and the publisher hereby disclaims any responsibility for them.

The author of this book does not dispense medical advice or prescribe the use of any technique as a form of treatment for physical, emotional, or medical problems without the advice of a physician, either directly or indirectly. The intent of the author is only to offer information of a general nature to help you in your quest for emotional and spiritual well-being. In the event you use any of the information in this book for yourself, which is your constitutional right, the author and the publisher assume no responsibility for your actions.

Any people depicted in stock imagery provided by Getty Images are models, and such images are being used for illustrative purposes only. Certain stock imagery © Getty Images.

Print information available on the last page.

ISBN: 978-1-9822-3406-5 (sc)
ISBN: 978-1-9822-3407-2 (e)

Balboa Press rev. date: 09/09/2019

CONTENTS

DEDICATION

To my Mother, Father, Grandparent,

Sialkot City, Pakistan which made me what I am today!

INTRODUCTION

God still does raises up men and women who perfectly fulfill their Spiritual Promise of recognizing the soul as a living reality within themselves and of experiencing the true love of God that transcends all and guard the fruits of the Spirit in themselves.

I am one such person. For forty plus years, I have personally experienced this oneness with God. This impression detached me entirely from the world and gave me such a great love for God that it hasn't changed in all of the forty years I have been walking with Him.

As God is my witness, I've always been aware of God's presence by talking with Him throughout each day. I nourish my soul by seeing God as *awareness* behind my own mind's thinking. It is called an awakening process which is the *separation* of the thinking of the mind and my *awareness* of the mind's thinking without being involved in it.

During the day, as I go about my daily business, and at night before I go to sleep I nourish my soul by seeing God in a state of extreme happiness and derive a great joy at being His. I give myself *totally* to God no matter what I have to sacrifice for it—even life itself.

My only happiness comes from doing God's will.

One easy way for me to succeed in giving myself to God as much He wants, I constantly guard my own soul because my soul is most certainly involved in both the spiritual as well as in the things of this world.

I always accept God's help and guard my soul according to His wishes this way I do commune with Him whenever I need to. When I am troubled by something, I very seldom seek any help about it. Knowing only that God is present.

And in God's love, I always find myself again. Thinking often spoils everything; the evil usually begins with my thoughts. I would reject any thoughts which distracts me from serving God or which undermine my exercises to maintain the presence of God in this *hectic* world.

Freeing the mind of such thoughts did permit a comfortable conversation with God. I must admit that it isn't always easy. The human mind is very powerful. It will do everything in its power to keep me away from the light of God because it is the dark side of human personality.

I learned to control my own mind simply by controlling my own thinking. As God is my witness, I can keep my own mind under my own full control 24/7 simply by controlling my own thinking.

You see, I have no control what-so-ever over what other people say, do or even thing but, I've full and complete control over what *I* think or what goes into my own mind. It is a God-given right and privilege for me. and also for everyone on the planet earth.

My 40+ YEAR's EXPERIENCE

For forty plus years, I have kept my own mind under my own full control by using positive self-suggestions and affirmations such as: ***Lord, I'm all yours. Do whatever you "will" with me. Or, "Lord, I receive, thank you for your presence.***

I keep repeating my positive affirmations until there is ***literally*** no time left for the mind to think on its own. For me, the secret of controlling my own mind is to ***bypass*** my own mind in order to ***free*** my own soul.

I have discovered that in all the holy books it is written that God blew His own Spirit into man and the man became a ***living*** human being. What that means in simple language is that ***I*** and everyone as a human being is divine part of God.

In other words, ***I am what God is. Just think of it!*** In the beginning a little effort was needed for me to form the habit of continuously ***conversing with God telling Him everything that was happening.***

Every once in a while, suddenly, I would have this deep inner urge to converse and talk with God and *praise* **Him** and thank Him for all the blessings He has already bestowed upon me.

As I contemplate on my past forty plus years talking and conversing with God, I Notice with profound interest that He did always surround and protect me and warned me from all upcoming dangers and informed me of the worldly and spiritual opportunities without my knowledge like magic.

Interestingly enough, after a brief practice to maintain the presence of God, God's love rejoices me, and moreover; it all became easy for me. One of the key thing I do is that whenever I want to do some good work, I always ask God for His help.

The funny thing is that immediately I would be given more than I asked for. One day, while I was walking in my parking lot at work, I shouted very loud, *I love you God—But, You know that.*

A woman nearby was also walking in that parking lot and heard me shouting aloud and gave me very strange look. **I guess that she must have thought that I was some crazy guy.** Suddenly, I told her, Madam, *I do talk to God and He listens.* **She gave me a big smile and kept on going.**

When I sinned, I always confessed to God with these words: *Lord, please help me overcome these mistakes I may correct them. After that I did not feel guilty about the sin.* And, I would continue to love God as before I sinned. After that, I did not dwell on the thoughts of heaven and hell.

Amazingly enough, my life was always filled with freedom and rejoicing. One of the key things I've learned by maintaining the presence of God is that only human beings are capable of recognizing the soul within us and of experiencing the deep, divine love of God that transcend all **including themselves.**

Human beings are sacred for that special reason.

If only you could understand that simple fact, you would never need to read another self-help book! How can we observe God when we are observing resentment or worry? **So—where is God?** God in goodness. If you want to find God, don't waste your time with what is,bad, spend your time in your goodness.

Once I enter the divine presence of God and maintain the God's presence I no longer worry about the past or the future. This is one key thing to remember.*The point is that only humans are capable of recognizing the soul within and of experiencing the divine love of God that transcend all things including themselves.*

I try to get above the experience as I maintain the presence of God. People ask me, ***What do you gain by learning how to maintain the presence of God?*** **I say to them, I am living in the eternity right here right now.**

I've full awareness of my soul dwelling a sort of **unwillingly** on the negative realms of Spirit and wanting to 'get-off" this 'time-track' **so that to reach and experience the positive realms of Spirit and into the Kingdom of Heaven.**

So—in a way, I'm doing what I will be doing for eternity. I have full and complete *awareness of myself as soul, not in just theory but as a daily living reality.* **I am also aware of my sins and, I am not at all surprised by them. I simply confess my sins to God, with begging Him to forgive without pleading with God or making any excuses.**

God knows human nature, remember He created humans as superior to all of His other creations before them. The funny thing is that after confession my sins to God, *I am able to peacefully resume my regular activity of love and adoration of God.* I also thank God if I didn't sin, because only God's grace could keep me from sinning.again.

Key to the success in this matter is that I try not to get fearful. Instead, I *feel* connected with God and see His presence. I start to praise God by saying: *"I love you God. Or Thank you God, do what you will with me.*

One thing I've noticed is that God love us to praise Him and thank Him for all His blessings. That is why I repeat my praises of God and thanking Him over and over again is that I know that God loves to hear me repeat those words.

As I've mentioned before that our mind's incessant, compulsive and repetitive and involuntarily thinking often spoils everything for me, that evil (mind) usually brings with my own thoughts.

I would try my level best to reject any thoughts, which distracted me from maintaining the presence of God or which underestimate my determination to 'hold' the mind quiet no matter what.

I knew for sure that *freeing* the mind of any such thoughts will make it possible for me a way for conversation with God. But, to be perfectly frank with you this wasn't always easy.

When I first started these daily exercises to maintain

the presence of God 24/7 no- matter what I often seemed to spend my entire 'spiritual exercises time' rejecting distractions and then falling immediately into them again. **It was indeed awful!**

As God is my witness, with practice and persistence, I did win over my mind. I must admit, it did take a big chunk of my forty year's trying to maintain the presence of God.

But, I'll tell you one thing that the feeling to win over mind is something that you never get tired of. I assure you. My own mind is under my own full and complete control 24/7, day or night, seven days a week, 365 days a year after year for forty plus years. **Just think of it!**

Imagine, how many people on the surface of the earth can honestly claim this on a daily bases. The fact is, my own mind would not dare *think* of anything, anytime day or night. Please understand that I don't tell you all this to impress you or to brag. Far from it! I tell you all this because if I can do it, anyone on earth can do it.

People want to know the technique of how to maintain the presence of God?

They want to know just how do you know if you are connected with God and having a heart-to-hear conversation? Well, I can only tell you how I do it. It is really simple when you know how?

THE FIRST STEP

The very first step is to do whatever it takes control your own mind simply by controlling your own thinking.

You see, the human mind, as power and as Vast it is, the fact is that mind cannot occupy or 'hold' two *thoughts* simultaneously at the same time. Only one though must occupy the mind at any given time. Either you control the mind with your own positive self-suggestions -- or the mind controls it with its negative useless repetitive and involuntary thoughts.

There is no half way in between. My goal in step one is to conquer my own mind and bypass it in order to *free* my soul and become a divine part of Spirit (God). For me, it has really become an *awakening* process which is the *separation of the thinking of the mind and my awareness of the mind's thinking.* It is as if the mind is dead (so to speak)

In the East, it's called the **"no-mind"** or a **mind without any thoughts.** The word no-mind, as I refer to here, simply means **a quiet mind** as if the mind is dead (so to speak).

In other words, it is a *'state-of-mind'* in which *You* become totally *aware* of *yourself* as Soul—*not in just theory* but, living reality in your daily life. Suddenly, you 'feel' lifted to a sense of higher spiritual elevation.

THE SECOND STEP

Step two is that I begin to feel as if l I am truly living in the reality of "this- moment", **right here right now.**

There are no-thoughts of the past. The future does not exist. I am living in the eternity, right here and right now in "this-moment". Time just seemed to stand still or just vanish in thin air. **I've full awareness of my soul dwelling in the Kingdom of Heaven.**

I close my eyes, and start to visualize myself conversing and talking with God. I start by saying: *I love you God— but, you know that.* Suddenly, it brings a big smile on my face. I sense as if God loves to hear me to keep repeating these words of praise and gratitude for all the blessing He has already bestowed upon me since my birth, God has always surrounded and protected me against any harmful diseases or sickness.

When people tell me that they have a migraine "head-ache", I have no clue as to what in the heck they are talking about. **Am I super human**? Of course not? I am just an average person just like you.

The only difference is that I have taken full and complete possession of my own mind and directed to toward my burning desire to maintain the presence of God and have a heart-to-heart talk with God 24/7 and to continually to praise Him and show my gratitude for all the blessing God has already, bestowed upon me.

NO SPECIAL SKILLS NEEDED

The most amazing thing is that I do not need any special or unique skills or any advance knowledge or university degree to go to God. **Just think of it!**All that is necessary for me is **my heart committed** entirely and completely to God out of my love and devotion for God above all others, nothing else. That's it.

Now here's my own confession: *I love God, more than anything or anyone in the whole wide world.* **WOW!**

What's the word God?

The word "God", in the way I refer here simply means the *awareness* of myself that I see and *feel* within me *as who I am in reality. Not my own physical body— instead a spiritual entity within me that blinks my eyes, breaths in and out of my body and, keeps the circulation of my blood flowing through-out my heart.*

And, what do I have to give in return for all these God's blessings? **You got it.** *All that is necessary for me is my* *heart committed entirely and completely to God out of my love for God above all others, nothing else.* That's it. I believe its bargain. Don't you!

Over the past forty-five years

Over the past forty plus years, trying to maintain the presence of God, one major thing I've noticed with profound interest and that is nothing is more pleasing to God more than to always be *aware* of God's presence by *talking* with Him throughout each day.

As God is my witness, for the past forty plus years, I have conversation with God 24/7. Day or night, seven days a week 365 days a year after year for forty plus years and counting. **One thing I have noticed is that God appreciates our gratitude and thanking Him with love and devotion for all His blessings.**

The reason I say this is that every time I show my gratitude to God, I suddenly 'feel' a tiny pressure of 'tingle' **in my head** as if something or someone has made a connection *spiritually* and I sense a joy all over me.It hits me like a jolt of lightening—**Wham!**

A CLEAR SIGN FOR ME

It is clear sign for me that I am one with God.

There are several ways for me to show my gratitude to God. Here is the one I say most: ***Thank you O' God for giving me the opportunity of recognizing the Soul within me and of experiencing of your deep and true love that transcend all.***

TO SUM UP

To sum up let me say this that: if you remember nothing else just remember this that : **You and I and every human being on the planet earth is a Soul, a divine part of God. This is our permanent relationship with our creator God.**

HERE IS AN EXAMPLE

if you have very large glass of water and you pour some in a very small cup, what will have in the small

cup? You'll still have the same water but in a small cup. The same way, God could be the water in large glass and humans in a small cup. So, God can be ike the water in the large glass while humans are the same water in a small cup. Get the picture?

Here's another example of relationship with one Creator God.

If you take a tiny drop of water from the ocean, it will still have all the faculties of the water in the ocean but it's not the ocean itself. The same way God is sort of the ocean (so the speak) but we human are tiny drops of the water in the ocean.

The point I'm trying to convey here is that all these drops of water from the ocean has all the qualities and attributes of the vast ocean but not the ocean. The ocean can be a sort of the creator God and the each drop can be considered as the human.

Another example is the Sun with billions of bright

shining tiny rays but each ray is not the Sun but a part of the Sun. **But, I think, you get the picture.**

In closing, Let me emphasize what I've discovered about how to succeed in life by giving myself *totally* to God by constantly maintaining the presence of God. I must constantly guard my Soul.

During my forty plus years of working with my Soul as a divine part of God what I've ultimately discovered is that a **Soul is involved in the spiritual matters as much as in the worldly matters.**

Try not to miss this point.

If I have not become *aware* of myself as Soul—God will not answer my call. This I know for sure. I can commune with God whenever I like. I must give myself *totally* to God. There is no half way in between.

In the next chapter, we will discuss: ***How I Maintain the Presence of God?*** I ask that you go right ahead and read the next chapter.

CHAPTER ONE

How I Maintain the Presence of God?

As God is my witness, most of my adult life, I have been given the opportunity of recognizing the soul within me and experiencing the deep, true love of God that transcends all. I didn't understand it. I thought that I was going crazy.

So—I just kept quiet on the subject. The reason is that I feared that I will be misunderstood if I shared my inner experiences with others. I mean to say that how do you go about explaining other people that I see this world as an illusion and I see all people as if on the motion picture screen.

I made perfect sense, and held an intelligent conversation with others but, to me it was as if 'someone' else was doing the talking. I often wondered about my 'identity-structure' of my personality.

I would sense as if there is a part of me that is **not** physical but instead it is spiritual that dwells inside of me and loves me and more importantly **longs** to communicate with me. Could this be God dwelling inside of me?

But, most of my life I was given the impression of God, as fearful God and we have to be punished for our sins. So, how can this God loving me and does long to communicate with me?

Then, suddenly I remember the **Adam, one of God's prophet** and how God blew His Spirit into his body and he became a living human being. Amazingly enough, suddenly, this 'non-physical' part inside of me began to make a perfect sense, at least to my own satisfaction.

All the holy books of God call this spiritual part dwelling within all of us as the Soul the divine part of God. Sure enough, I began to see and feel this soul within me as an *'awareness'* of myself within me as a soul, *not* just in 'theory' but, living reality in my daily life.

I became *aware* of myself as a soul within me and began to give myself *totally* to God in both the physical and the spiritual affairs. My only happiness and joy began to come from doing God's will. God helps and guards my soul according to His will. I began to commune with God 24/7 for forty plus years.

I must admit that a little effort was required to *form* the habit of continuously conversing with God., telling Him everything that was happening but after a little practice, it became a second nature for me.

I have always consulted with God about everything. I praise Him 24/7. I show my gratitude and thank Him for every blessing He bestow upon me. When I sin I confess it to Him and ask for His forgiveness for the mistake without feeling guilty about it. I know the flesh is week but the spirit is willing to do good deeds.

So—the foundation of my spiritual life began as the

faith which revealed to me the joyful position of God. As it became secure in the depths of my heart, everything became easy to live in the thoughts of God and able to do for the love of God.

I truly began to understand that the perfect faith in God is a great honor to God, and gave Him a 'open-door' to answer my questions and send blessings upon me.

But, perhaps the most wonderful benefit of communion with God is that it taught me to surrender myself entirely to God, resolving to do anything for God and He always protected me and not allow me to suffer through trails for very long, but gave me a way of escape that I might endure—every-time.

During the time that has passes, my heartfelt goal has been to *think* of nothing but God. If I didn't have time to think of God I did not become upset about it. Eventually I came up with a simple technique that allowed me to think of God 24/7 day and night seven days a week and 365 days a year after year for forty plus years till present.

Interestingly enough, this simple technique showed me how to maintain the Presence of God in this **hectic** world.

HOW TO SPLIT THE MIND IN TWO HALVES?

What I do is that during the day as I go about my business, I **split** my own mind into two halves. With one half of the mind, I do my all worldly activities such as running my business, conversation with other people, answering the phones, driving my car, taking kids to school, eating food, writing this book and so on.

And, with other half of my mind I do all my spiritual activities such as doing my spiritual exercises, reading my spiritual books, conversation with God, visualizing my spiritual goals as already achieved, showing my gratitude to God and saying thanks to God for all the blessings He has bestowed upon me and so on.

Now—you may be wondering at this very moment that just how in the world I can **split** the mind into two halves?

If you are then let me share with you how I do it. I

believe and you will concur that it is true technique to split the mind in two halves. Let me explain.

Ever ***notice*** that whenever you are listening to a lecture or sermon in church or in a class or a seminar, you maybe ***"doodling"*** something on a blank sheet of paper?

Perhaps, you are drawing a picture on a blank sheet of paper or writing something about a goal or a "to do list" after the lecture or the sermon.

What you have done is to ***split*** the mind into two halves (so to speak). With one half of the mind, you are perfectly listening to the lecture or the seminar and with other half of the mind you are drawing a beautiful photo or taking notes.

So—the same way, during the day as I go about my daily business I can do my all worldly activities with one part of mind and have a heart-to-heart conversation with my creator God with the second part of the mind.

It's hard to do when you start but become easy with practice. Then, at night, before I go to sleep, with one half on the mind I try to quiet the mind and with the other half of the mind I thank God with my own positive affirmations.

It's a feeling that I can never get tired of while I maintain the presence of God. It has become a sort of a holy ritual for me. The sad thing is that 80-90 percent of all population has no *clue* whatsoever about this divine part of God known as Soul within us.

Over the past forty plus years while practicing how to maintain the presence of God, what I have learned, without any room for doubts is that in order to succeed in giving myself 100 percent to God as much as God wants I must constantly guard my own soul.

The problem is that when I go to see the soul, I mostly see my 'thought' and nothing else.

The reason that I cannot see the soul is because my soul is wrapped up in me.

The human mind as strong and powerful as it may sometimes seem it isn't—The Soul is solid ground.

In all honesty, I can say that I feel much closer to God

in this day-to-day activities than most people ever believe possible. For more than forty years, my principal endeavor has been to stay as close as possible to God, doing, saying, and even thinking nothing that might displease God.

To be perfectly honest with you, I have no other reason except to show my deep gratitude for God's pure love, and mostly because God deserves infinitely more than that— anyway! I can also admit and confess that I have become so accustomed to God's Divine presence.

It would be an understatement to say that my own soul has been filled with a constant inner joy and happiness that is so overwhelming, I feel compelled to do what may seem to some as **childish** things. I always, without fail, rely on God's help on all kinds of occasions.

Sometimes I suddenly have the strong urge to respond to God's calling. By offering my heart to God, by tender loving look and by constantly offering my words: ***I love you God—but, you know that.***

I get a big smile on my face—as if God received it.

Sadly enough, whenever I mention the word, Soul to my friends, associates or world leaders, they seem to have no clue to what I am talking about. No matter how intellectual or intelligent a person may be in book learning wise,he or she seem to be un-aware of the soul or **who we are** as a human beings.

A True Story

I remember quiet vividly, that during my undergraduate studied at the Columbia College in Los Angeles, California I went to see the president of that college Dr. Earnest Baumaster who was one of the California's highest rated vocational colleges and told him that I have a personal problem and wanted his help.

He said, sure, come to my office anytime, and he will help. I made an appoint to see him and met with him in high floor plush office. I asked him, that sometimes, I see people as if they are on a motion picture screen and not associated with me.

I explained to him it is as if someone else inside of me

doing the talking and not me. I asked him what he thought about it. The president of my college was considered highly intelligent and intellectual in worldly sense. He was also the President of several other highly successful communication based vocational colleges in America. so, naturally I expected a wise answer from him about my personality situation.

But on the contrary to my expectations, the answer he gave me sort of surprised me, to say the least. Here's is what the president said. ***Mr. Jaafri, I believe you do have a deep problem with the "identity-structure" structure of your personality. In your own mind, you think that you have a "dual" personality. I highly recommend you see a "head-shrink".*** (Whatever it means).***He said that he has a doctor friend who he can make an appointment for me who can help.***

Later I found out the word "head-shrink" he was referring to is called the ***Psychiatrist.*** The whole point I am trying so hard to make is that no matter how intelligent you may be or how intellectual you may be book knowledge wise, you may not have any clue as to *who you are* as a human being.

The fact is that we are a Soul, a Divine part of God. As such, we are *a physical- being* as well as *spiritual being.* There are two distinct personalities within each of us. One is that we see when we stand before a mirror. This is our physical self.

And the other is that we do not normally see when we stand in front of a mirror but rather we *"assume"* or see and feel *inside* of us. This is the self that blinks your eyes, controls the circulation of your blood in your heart, runs your mind, and breaths *in and out* like a clock-work. But mostly, this is your spiritual self that hold perfect conversation with God. Is it any wonder why I maintain the presence of God as part of daily living.

Let me share a true story to explain how ignorant we are when it comes to knowing *who we are* and what our whole purpose in life is for having given us the opportunity to live this life as a physical and spiritual beings here on the planet earth.

Please understand that I am not a very religious person but I do consider myself as a very spiritual person. Religions are rituals we do but—Spiritual is *who we are.* **There is distinct difference between the two.** So—here's the true story.

Not too long ago, I received a postcard from the director of one of the world's largest health care organizations in California. This postcard from the director of this health care organization has a message written on it. It said: *There is no prophet in curing the body if in the process you destroy the Soul.*

When I read this message on the postcard, I said to myself: *How can you destroy* Something that is Divine and a part of God? You cannot destroy the Soul. Period! This highly intellectual, highly intelligent, well meaning director had no clue as to who we are as a physical and a spiritual human beings created in the image of God by God.

So—the big question is that how do you go about becoming *aware* yourself as Soul not in just theory but, a living reality in your daily living and maintain the presence of God.

What I share with you in this book is not some 'hearsay', or just theory or something impossible to do for an average person. Every word I say to you in this book is 'living' proof of the validity of how I maintain the presence of God by my conversation with God. I don't say that it will be quiet easy to do or a piece of cake (so to speak) for you to do because it will not be true.

Nothing worthwhile in life ever comes easy. You can bet on that. It will not come to those who are not consciously searching for it. All I can say is try it. If it works for you do it and if it does not work for you just let go of it. That's exactly the attitude I have toward my own spiritual progression.

If it does not work for you it does not necessarily mean that you failed. It can only mean that you are not as ready for such spiritual knowledge at this particular time. Remember, it took forty plus long years before I could recognize the Soul within and the true love of God.

There are some key things that that are clear sign for me to indicate that I am in the presence of God in "this-moment" right here right now and all I have to do is to maintain the presence of God in "this-moment".

For example, during those moments when I feel the presence of God within, I begin to sense a tiny 'tingle' or pressure in my head and I am lifted to a higher level of spiritual elevation.

The funny this is that, while writing this manuscript, I am feeling these quiet, silent *tingle* like pressure in my head. at this very moment.

SEEING WORLD AS AN ILLUSION

What happens next is that I begin to sense this physical world as an *illusion.* Please don't get me wrong. What I really mean is that I feel as if I see the physical world through my "other- self" the spiritual self within me.

If I am driving on the road, suddenly I see the palms

tree and road signs as a ***"multidimensional-awareness"*** of nature on that road and I am a part of the nature.

Metaphysically speaking, seeing the physical world simply means that as of my ***Spiritual-self*** is seeing the nature on the road and my own ***Physical-self*** is just driving the car. On the road. I don't know I got home.

All I remember is saying out aloud: ***Lord, I receive. Thank you for your presence.*** I declare that God is one with me as I am one with Him in "this- moment" right here right now.

The key thing is that after forty plus years of the practice of the presence of God and trying to maintain it has made it possible for me to vividly see and feel the presence of God within me. Don't get me wrong.

I don't just see or feel God in the physical body. I just can't, because God is ***Spirit***, and can only see and feel God in my ***Spirit***. All conversation is done intuitively through my spirit-body. If the physical world is just an illusion then what purpose does it serve for people?

Spiritual Masters of all ages have confirmed without any room for doubt that the physical world serves a "training-ground" for the soul to learn all attributes of God. It is a school (so to speak) where soul learn 'self-realization' and ultimately Soul gains God-Realization and eventually returns home to God in Heaven from where It came from.

During my forty plus years is my conversation with God the key thing I've learned is that I came into this physical world attempting to fulfill certain qualities in myself.

I went about it in many ways. I finally figured it out that *I am here to find out who I am and to find out were my home in Spirit is, and go there in consciousness and have a heart-to-heart talk with God.* I believe this is my whole purpose on the planet earth. The sad thing is that you and I don't belong here spiritually.

I was put in this body and most of things I want don't function here because our intention only function in the Spirit.

The key thing I've learned is that my mind is my enemy

because it will go against me in my Sprit. And it seems to win. When I did find the true me, and I am really living that life, I did find out I don't care whether I live and die because that part of me will always exist.

Suddenly, I stopped fearing poverty because I found the wealth from the Spirit inside of me and became quiet well-off during my life. I try not to let my thoughts, feelings or ego move me. I let my heart move me. Sometimes, it will tell me a little bit ahead of time, and other times it will just walk me into it and see how I handle it.

But with Spirit with me, I won't be given what cannot be handled. I do see each challenge as an opportunity to test and develop my talents impeccably. When I am truly alive and joyful I'm awake, negative power cannot trap me. To trap me it has to find a negative pattern.

The great deal of the stress that people suffer is a result of not living right now, of being occupied with the past or the future. I believe this is the cause of so many troubles. I try my level best to cut out my concern for the future and my remembrance of the past.

In the next chapter, we will discuss: ***How I hold the Presence of God*** I ask that you jump right into this chapter. Two while it's still fresh in your m

CHAPTER TWO

How I hold the Presence of God?

The worse trial I could ever imagine is losing my sense of God's presence, which has been with me for forty plus years. But my own confidence in God's grace and goodness makes me certain that God would never leave me entirely.

One easy way I've found to hold the God's presence is that I must constantly guard my own soul. Interestingly enough, I found myself quiet well-off. Everything I ever desired or wanted just seem to come from nowhere. The most important part of holding the presence of God lay in renouncing, once for all, whatever does not lead to God.

This allows me to become involved in a continuous conversation with God in a simple and unhindered manner. All I do is to recognize my soul within me and the deep love of God that transcend all. What's more I continually ***affirm*** God as being intimately present within me.

Then, I speak directly to God every time I need to ask for help, to know His 'will' in moments of troubles or uncertainty, and to do whatever God wants me to do that pleases Him.

My continuous conversation with God also includes praising and thanking and loving God incessantly for His infinite goodness and perfection. I ask confidently for God's grace in everything I say do or even think. My soul is always resting in God, having lost its ***awareness*** of everything but love of God.

My prayers consisted ***totally*** and simply of God's presence. My practice of the presence of God has truly become enjoyable habit. It has become a reflex. thanking God, praising God, talking with God 24/7 has become a real habit for me. In the morning, as I drive to work, I habitually start saying to myself: ***I love you God—but, you know that.***

Suddenly a big smile comes on my face and I am lifted to higher level of spiritual elevation and I sense the presence of God all over me. Because of this my own life is always full of continual joy and happiness. I never get tired of doing even the smallest things for God.

The practice cause my effort to become a pleasurable habit that I do it without thinking. For more than forty years, my own major goal has been to stay as close to God as possible, doing, saying, and mostly thinking nothing but God.

I have no other reason for doing this, except to show his gratitude for God's pure love, and because I believe that God deserves infinitely more than that anyway.

For forty plus years I've become so accustomed to God's divine presence that I rely on it for help on all sort of matters. My soul has been filled with a constant inner joy that is always so overwhelming, I feel an urge to do things what may seem to some as childish things.

Once I was driving on the road and suddenly I yelled out

aloud, ***"My Lord, I am all yours, do what YOU will with me."*** I notice that police car was driving on the lane next to me. The police man looked at me and said, ***Is everything OK?"*** The policeman was just surprised as I was and we both laughed. (No ticket was Given to me for yelling so aloud on open road.).

Experiencing these things makes me certain beyond any doubts that God is always in the depth of my Soul, no matter what I do or what happens to me. Then, it is almost as if ***this God of love*** returns to my own soul to rest again, satisfied with these few words.

You are about to become aware of a spiritual 'secret' that may change your whole life-style completely, just it has mine. I have taken the liberty, my dear friends, of telling you all this so you might re-examine your own relationship with God. I can honestly tell you that nothing has influenced my own life more than my first enthusiasm and love for God. I'm not well-known, in worldly terms, but with God I am tenderly loved and caressed.

But, before you and I become involved in this intricate and unique way to transform your own life, let's first, have a 'heart-to-heart' talk. ***I'll talk and you will listen, okay.***

A few years ago, through my own mistake and stupidity, and an offer for a business venture in the Middle-East, I lost everything that was precious to me, my home, my belonging and my business.

Down on my luck and no place to go to, I began to wander around, searching for myself and some answers that would make my own life bearable. I spent much time in local parts and in public libraries because they were warm and free. Hoping to find a royal road to riches and fortunes, I joined several 'secret- fraternal" organizations.

Day-by-day, I began to sink deeper and deeper into depression. I was totally broke: financially and emotionally and especially spiritually. Then, Just out of depression, I made some drastic changes.

And, the way I made these drastic changes was that instead of feeling sorry for myself and blaming all others for my own faults and misfortunes, I decided to totally commit myself by reading as many motivational, self-help and personal development books, tapes. CD's, DVD's and seminars classes and courses as I could find.

Frankly, I didn't really know what I was looking for. But for some reasons I felt as if I will find it because, *of the principle of Seek and it will be Given unto you.* So-to make a long story short, my passion, my mission, my obsession had become to find out what really was the one key 'secret' of all successful people in all walks of life.

I wanted to know the difference between me and all other people who were successful in life. I wanted to know the one foundation key 'secret' to all human success and achievement. Interestingly enough, at that moment in my life, the measure of success was limited only to personal material and professional success. I had no interest in spirituality at that time of the failure in the business venture in the middle.

Frankly, for forty plus years talking with God has

become one single *"act'* of my daily prayers that *never* ends. This is what I do for eternity.

I have now learned to cultivate the deep presence of God so thoroughly in my heart that I am blessing God, praising Him, adoring Him, and loving Him with all my heart. For more than forty years, this practice of the presence of God has given me both blessing and inspiration for knowing God in all His majesty and feeling His loving presence throughout each simple day.

THE PHYSICAL WORLD IS AN ILLUSION

All those who have the good fortune of practicing the art and science of the presence of God and have already "experience" intuitively some degree of the presence of God in their own daily live do agree with me that:

Tthis state- of -the presence of God is nothing more nor less than seeing the physical world as an illusion, the nature becoming a multidimensional "awareness". and of recognizing that the soul within and experiencing the deep love of God within".

CHAPTER THREE

How I must seek first the Kingdom of Heaven Then, all else will be added unto us!

Perhaps, you too, like me have often wondered that what does that phrase really mean to us as a human being living on earth?

Does that mean that I must **have** the *Kingdom of Heaven* first, and then all else will be given to me? But, as I read the passage again, it does not say that at all it says *seek,* not *have*. There is a big difference between **having** and *seeking* The point is that when I *seek,* the Kingdom of Heaven *first*, that is when I discover this *"Kingdom of Heaven"* **Get the picture?**

Few people knew it, but I seek, the "Kingdom of Heaven"

first, the **energy** the 'creative-imagination' out of the great **cesspool** of the consciousness comes within me. One of the most wonderful gifts from our creative is the faculty of the 'creative-imagination.

No other creation of God has this unique privilege except us—as human beings. Through the power of the 'creative-imagination' only human beings are capable of **observing** the presence of God in all things, including themselves. ***Human beings are sacred for that very reason.*** Just think of it!

All those who intuitively understand the power of the 'creative-imagination' do agree with me that they never need to read another self-help book! I believe, and I am sure you concur that how can we observe God when we are observing resentment or worry?

HOW I SEEK FIRT THE KINGDOM OF HEAVEN?

Introduction to the Realms of Spirit.

Let me be perfectly honest with you and tell you that this biblical verse ***Seek first, the Kingdom of Heaven then, all*** *else will be added onto you,* (Mathew 6:30) in the way I use here refers to my own experience of visualizing the realms of Spirit in my own imagination during my daily spiritual exercises,meditation and self-examinations sessions on a daily basis.

I believe that all those who have already *intuitively* experienced these realms of Spirit *beyond* the physical realm, do agree with me that there are spiritual worlds *beyond the physical world. (earth).*

Spiritual Masters of all ages have declared that there are **'thirty**-three' realms of Spirit, **and the physical realm is just one of them.** They *affirm* that six of these spiritual realms namely: *physical, astral, causal, mental, etheric and Soul* exist in the physical realm simultaneously at the same time.

And, the other **'twenty-seven' realms of spirit** all have the positive *aspect* of the *astral,* **causal, mental, etheric, and Soul there.** What I have learned is that the key thing to notice here is that only in the physical level do all six levels exists simultaneously at the same time.

The Soul realm is the only positive *aspect* and carries through all the other realms of spirit. I imagine, or visualize, or just pretend that the Soul realm is the first of the positive realms of existence. And, the 'twenty-seven' ascending realms of Spirit above the Soul ream.

Interestingly enough, realms of Spirit *below* the Soul realms are 'training- ground' (so to speak) for human self-realization—and the realms of Spirit *above* the Soul realm—are for the *God-Realization.* Nothing has influenced my own life more than knowing the full signification of the creation by God.

It has truly given me the total understanding of the Soul as the most important aspect and carries through in—**everything**—meaning the Soul, that *"I Am".* It is *who I really am.*

It took me forty plus years to gain through my own experience of going into various realms of Spirit. I share it here with you to know ***not*** something for you to just memorize it and learn only ***mentally*** but as background that you ***can*** have should you choose to practice your own ***"inner-travels"***.

In the East from where I come from, it's called the ***Soul-travel."*** The point is that you can know all these "thirty-three' realms of Spirit through your own ***direct*** experience, at which point the information moves out of the theoretical area and becomes experiential. It certainly has for me. For more detailed information on the subject log on: www.msia.org. A world's most major source of this information.

MAINTAINING THE PRESENCE OF GOD

For me, all my own spiritual life came by maintaining the practice of the presence of God 24/7 and I earnestly believe from the bottom of my heart that anyone who practices it with persistence and devotion and in faith will eventually, ***fulfill their spiritual promised.***

To accomplish this for forty plus long years it was necessary for me to empty my own mind of everything that would offend God. **God wants to possess my heart and mind completely.** I believe that before any work can be done in my own Soul, God *must* be totally in control there isn't any half way in between.

For me, there isn't any sweeter way of blissful living in the physical realm than my continuous-communion with God. I believe, that only those who intuitively *Seek* (not have) *first the kingdom of Heaven* are the ones *to whom all else will be added onto them.*

I must say that that you don't practice, the presence of God for the sole purpose of gaining consolation for your problems. I believe that you should *Seek it, rather, than worrying to have it first, because God want it from—us— out of love for God.* This understanding alone turned my own life for good.

How hard is it for us to understand?

Sometimes, I indulge in my own imagine to see what kind of a place this world would be in which to live if all the preachers of the world, regardless of the religious beliefs would preach nothing but practicing the presence of God. Because I do believe it will surely be responsible for guiding souls in the right direction.

By way of this book, I would urge everyone to be *aware of God's constant presence.* If for no other purpose than because God' presence is a delight to my own soul and spirit—the divine part of God. If we do practice the presence of God, I believe that one thing will be for sure that is I know how much I need God's grace and I would never lose the *touch of greatnes*s with my God.

For forty plus years, I have made a commitment *never* ever deliberately stray from God, and to live the rest of my own life in God's holy presence. One thing is for sure, I don't ever practice the presence of God in expectation of getting any heavenly comforts; I simply do it out of my deep love of God that transcend all.

TO SUM UP

So—to sum up everything let me ask you a quick question?

What does that really mean to you? **That you must <u>seek</u> first the Kingdom of Heaven then, all the rest will be added unto you.** Does that mean that you must *have* the Kingdom of Heaven first and then all the rest will be given to you? But read this phrase again. It does not say that at all. It says <u>*seek*</u>, not <u>*have*</u>.

So the big question is that what *does* happen to you and me and every other human beings on earth when we all *seek* first? For my own research while writing this manuscript I did a Google search to know the difference between the *Kingdom of Heaven* and the *Kingdom of God*, here's what I found out on that website.

For forty plus years, throughout my spiritual search I had to confront my own Mind. It is an enemy to all my highest intentions. It's like the little devil inside me that sits on my shoulder and whispers to me. It tells me all the negative things about the world, about other people. It tell me how bad they really are. It tells me the terrible things they do.

If you practice the presence of God, all this will gradually become familiar, and the way to seeking the **Kingdom of Heaven** and of the **Kingdom of God** will become second nature to you as it has for me for forty plus years. If the **awareness** of the presence of God is not maintained, you will lose it again.

But always remember, you have fallen asleep once do not fool yourself—you can fall asleep again. What I have learned is that I cannot permanently alienated and separated from God so I will lose my sense of the presence of God. I feel a yearning inside me, a loneless when I am with people; I will feel alienated and separated, as if I am not a part of what is going on around me.

Once I had begun on my own journey of spiritual progression, and had found that, totally spontaneously something happened to me. I still do not know as yet what really happened to me, but something occurred to lift me *above myself and brought me closer to God.*

All those who have intuitively done some amount of

Soul travel, do agree with me that when you maintain this practice of the presence of God—this experience can be as *deep*, as *ecstatic,* as *God-intoxicated* as you want it be.

I *trust* I have made it clear that as a Soul, a divine part of God, I *never* try to control the *guilt* the *separation*, and the rest. All I have to do is to recognize God as being in control and intimately present within me.

Then I may speak directly to Him every time I need to ask for help.

Many people have asked me. *By what authority do I speak? After all, I'm mere a minister and not anyone official or special. Yet I could ask, By what authority do you question? The authority to question and to speak out is both inherent within each one of us. I say what I say because I can.*

My spiritual teacher Rev. John-Roger, modern-day founder of the Movement of Spiritual Inner Awareness based in Los Angeles, California USA, has taught me that

his is a form of spiritual immunity, and it holds us back from our best selves.

Strangely enough, Once, I became spiritually mature, suddenly, I became ***attuned*** to my Soul nature. And I became totally ***aware*** of myself as Soul, not in theory, but a living reality in my daily living. The world became a screen where I project myself

WORLD IS AN ILLUSUIN

For the first time in my own life, I could recognize, relate, assimilate and apply what exactly it means when we say that ***the physical world is an illusion.***

In Closing, let me Just say this. Spending time in God's presence does not weaken the physical body. In fact, God won't allow any soul that is searching for Him to be comforted anywhere other than Him.

It has been very true for me, and I am a living proof this truth.

I also, feel that since I have such a short time to live in the physical world, I do want to spend my remaining

time with God while alive here on earth. I train myself to show my love for God by asking for His grace. I offer my heart to Him at every moment,

My preference has always been to retire with God to the deepest part of my soul as often as possible.

Before ending this chapter, I wish to share with you some of the most dramatic benefits I've personally received by practicing the presence of God as far as *How I seek first, the Kingdom of Heaven then all things are added onto me.*

BENEFITS OF SEEKING THE KINGDOM OF HEAVEN

Frankly, the benefits I've received are too numerous to mention in one volume book, but I'll try to share the ones that have truly changed my whole life from a failure to success, from a non-believer to a believer in the presence of God, from an arrogant person to a humble person, from a negative thinking to a positive thinking person, from a material minded to a spiritual-minded person.

And the list goes on and on, but, I think that you get the picture. I truly became vividly *"aware* "of the spiritual phenomenon that: ***If I can change my spiritual consciousness, I can spend more of my time in spiritual pursuit, instead of just re-acting to the material world. In other words, I can remain at peace 24/7.***

With this profound spiritual insight in the human psyche, I realized that ***I can never ever control God, but I can 'align' and flow with God's 'will'.*** For me, it's the one monumental key insight to holding the presence of God anytime, anywhere, day or night 24/7, 365 days a year after year till I die.

My own "Self-Realization" that as a human being ***I'm a Spiritual-being having a physical experience in a physical-body here on earth became evidence to my by my daily practice of the Presence of God.***

Now as spiritual-being I began to become *aware* of myself as Soul not, in theory but, a divine part of God in my daily life. As spiritual-being, I became capable of

Soul-travel through the lower six realms of Spirit, *physical, astral, causal, mental, etheric and Soul.*

My procedure was simply this. As I go to sleep, I would close my eyes, and imagine, or visualize or just pretend that as if I was in my **Soul-body**, and slowly moving upward from the physical, astral, causal, mental, etheric and the soul realms of Spirit.

By this spiritual exercise, I was *imagining* myself *inside* my own physical body. Then, I would visualized myself *outside* my body and now I am again moving upward in my spiritual body again but this time, from the *astral, causal, mental, etheric and the Soul realms of Spirit.*

The key thing to remember is that there are two Kingdoms, one inside the body and the other outside the body. One is the Kingdom of Heaven and the other is the Kingdom of God.

I do believe from the bottom of my heart, that most inventors, deep-thinking people, well-known artists, scientists, filmmakers find there knowledge from visiting these realms of Spirit, This book came from ***inner-knowledge*** not from me.

But, perhaps, the most significant benefit of the practice of the presence of God came about by the ***discovery*** and the ***revelation*** of the practice the way to ***Stalking the Spirit.***

Let me explain!

If I had only one day left on earth to live how would I want to spend it? Perhaps it is a silly question, but for me it's worth spending some time thinking about it. I reasoned that since I don't know the exact moment I am going to die, so I can ***forgive*** myself and pray and ***focus*** on the presence of God and say, ***Lord, I did the best I could.***

At the moment of my death, I would better start now. Suddenly, I was starting to see ***how precious is the time I have already have?*** And how much more precious is the time that remains to me? Please believe me when I tell you that keeping death in mind is ***not*** being morbid? It is simply being ***aware,*** that I do not have time to waste, that's all.

That is why, it is absolutely necessary to always be

aware of God's presence by talking with Him throughout each day. I must give myself *totally* to God, in both worldly and spiritual affairs.

After that I did not dwell on *thoughts* of heaven or hell because *thinking* often spoils everything that *evil* usually begins with our thoughts. In my opinion, I should *reject* any *thoughts* which undermine my practice the presence of God. Freeing the mind of such *thoughts* usually permit me a comfortable conversation with God.

But, in all honesty, it isn't always easy. In the beginning, I had often spent my entire spiritual meditation time rejecting distractions and then falling immediately into them again.

When I surrender myself entirely to God, resolving to do anything for God, the Lord always protected me from deception. God never allowed me to suffer through trials for longer than I could handle, but always gave me a way of escape that I might endure. For forty plus years my heartfelt goal has been to *think* of nothing but God.

If I did allow some time to pass without *thinking* of

God, I did not grow upset about it. Once I confessed my weakness to God, I just returned to God with all the more confidence and joy because I had found myself so unhappy apart from God's presence.

I found much closer to God in my day-to-day activities. With this assurance, I was **never** afraid of dying because complete surrender to God's 'will' is the only secure road to follow. In it, there is always enough **Light** to ensure safe travel.

One key thing for me is that no special knowledge or talent or any skill in necessary to go to God. For me all that is necessary is a heart dedicated entirely and solely to God out of **love** for Him.

All I have to do is to recognize, relate, assimilate and apply God as being intimately **present** within me. Then, I can speak directly to God every time I do need to ask for help, to know His 'will' in my own moments of uncertainty, and do whatever God wants me do in a way that pleases Him.

I often thank God for giving me the privilege and the

43

opportunity to live this life as a human being and live in the way He intended for me to be, I always thank God for the opportunity of recognizing my own Soul within and of experiencing His deep *love* that transcend all. I do declare as often as possible that ***Lord, I did the best I could.***

Perhaps you can now see why I say that I don't have much time to do anything other than focus on my purpose or intention. One thing I try my own level best to do is that try ***make peace with everyone. Why?*** Because everyone lives *inside* me!

I believe that ***how*** I die is so important to me because it will be my last ***thoughts*** **and** my own last *feelings* in this life. I mean what exactly my last words will be?

I also believe from the bottom of my own heart that how I handle my own ***turmoil,*** and ***existence*** during my last few moments is going to be very important to me because I believe that these few last moments in my life are going to determine my own ***placement*** in the realms of Spirit when I leave here.

So—those few last moment of my own life become very important to me. ***So— in a way, spiritually speaking, I say to myself that the life I've been living up to this moment on this planet has been a <u>rehearsal for my own death.</u>* Just think of it!**

I believe that idea of ***rehearsing*** my own death daily ***before*** I really die sort of made a lot sense to me. I reason, that ***repetition is the mother of skills.*** And, if I can find some spiritually charge ***affirmations*** then, I can start repeating them 24/7 day in and day out seven days a week and 365 day a year-after-year until I actually die and leave this planet.

The beauty of ***rehearsing*** my own final words ***prior to*** my own death will help me know exactly how I will get away from my body cleanly and where I'm going to place my own consciousness.

For me death now seems as natural as breathing and ***rehearsing*** my own death daily has become a second nature to me, a sort of a reflex that my mind is now habitually repeats my spiritually charged final words: ***Lord, I did the best I could.***

I call this for lack of proper words as ***Stalking the Spirit.*** I earnestly believe that this spiritual insight of ***rehearsing*** my death was added onto ***me*** by constantly ***Seeking both the Kingdom of Heaven and God."*** This I must do.

By my nightly ***"inner-travels in the realms of Spirit is*** as a part of rehearsal for my death. The key is never to stop searching until we have found it all! I don't know what God has in store for me, but I feel so serene and at peace 24/7 that it does not matter.

What do I have to be afraid of when I am one with God as He is with me. Lately, I don't know what's to become of me. It seems that a tranquil soul and a quiet spirit come to me even while I sleep. If I'm having hard time going to sleep I repeat my death ***rehearsal*** words silently and to myself until I do go to sleep.

Because I am at rest, the trails of life bring me no suffering because I know: *this too, shall pass.* I just

maintain the practice of the presence of God. I *know my mind is my own enemy because it will go against me in my Spirit.*

And it seems to win because although the Spirit, my Soul is very strong and Powerful the mind acts like a little devil sitting on my shoulder telling me how bad people and things are.

One easy way for me to prevent my mind from wandering away from God is to 'train' myself to dwell in God's presence all day long. This provide me a sort of "practice" for me, as I remind myself to concentrate on God.

Remaining in God's presence 24/7 thus becomes easier for me!

CHAPTER FOUR

How I Let God make perfect in me what was started

Let me share a few more benefits I have received by: ***How I Let God make perfect in me what was started by the understanding and the knowledge of the creation by God.*** I will just mention the few of the most dramatic things that were added onto me since I started the practice the present of God forty plus years ago.

The first thing that was added onto me was "Self-Realization" that as a human being ***I'm a Spiritual-being having a physical experience in a physical-body here on earth.***

Now as spiritual-being I began to become ***aware*** of myself as Soul not, in theory but, a divine part of God in my daily life. As spiritual-being, I became capable of Soul-travel through the lower six realms of Spirit, *physical, astral, causal, mental, etheric and Soul.*

My procedure was simply this. As I go to sleep, I would close my eyes, and imagine, or visualize or just pretend that as if I was in my Soul-body, and slowly moving upward from the physical, astral, causal, mental, etheric and the soul realms of Spirit.

By this spiritual exercise, I would *imagine* myself *inside* my own physical body. Then, I would visualized myself *outside* my body and now I am again moving upward in my spiritual body again but this time, from the *astral, causal, mental, etheric and the Soul realms of Spirit.*

The key thing to remember is that there are two Kingdoms, one inside the body and the other outside the body. One is the Kingdom of Heaven and the other is the Kingdom of God.

I do believe from the bottom of my heart, that most inventors, deep-thinking people, well-known artists, scientists, filmmakers find there knowledge from visiting these realms of Spirit. This book came from ***Inner-Knowledge*** not from me.

Suddenly, I was starting to see ***how precious is the time I have already have?*** And how much more precious is the time that remains to me? Please believe me when I tell you that keeping death in mind is ***not*** being morbid?

It is simply being ***aware,*** that I do not have time to waste, that's all. That is why, it is absolutely necessary to always be ***aware*** of God's presence by talking with Him throughout each day. I must give myself ***totally*** to God, in both worldly and spiritual affairs.

After that I did not dwell on ***thoughts*** of heaven or hell because ***thinking*** often spoils everything that ***evil*** usually begins with our thoughts. In my opinion, I should ***reject*** any ***thoughts*** which undermine my practice the presence of God. Freeing the mind of such ***thoughts*** usually permit me a comfortable conversation with God.

But, in all honesty, it isn't always easy.

In the beginning, I had often spent my entire spiritual meditation time rejecting distractions and then falling immediately into them again. When I surrender myself entirely to God, resolving to do anything for God, the Lord always protected me from deception.

God never allowed me to suffer through trials for longer than I could handle, but always gave me a way of escape that I might endure. For forty plus years my heartfelt goal has been to *think* of nothing but God. If I did allow some time to pass without *thinking* of God, I did not grow upset about it.

Once I confessed my weakness to God, I just returned to God with all the more confidence and joy because I had found myself so unhappy apart from God's presence. I found much closer to God in my day-to-day activities.

Then, I can speak directly to God every time I do need to ask for help, to know His 'will' in my own moments of uncertainty, and do whatever God wants me do in a way that pleases Him.

I often thank God for giving me the privilege and the opportunity to live this life as a human being and live in the way He intended for me to be, I always thank God for the opportunity of recognizing my own Soul within and of experiencing His deep *love* that transcend all. I do declare as often as possible that ***Lord, I did the best I could.***

Perhaps you can now see why I say that I don't have much time to do anything other than focus on my purpose or intention. One thing I try my own level best to do is that I try ***make peace with everyone. Why?*** Because everyone lives *inside* me!

I believe that *how* I die is so important to me because it will be my last ***thoughts*** **and** my own last ***feelings*** in this life. I mean what exactly my last words will be?

I also believe from the bottom of my own heart that how I handle my own ***turmoil,*** and ***existence*** during my last few moments is going to be very important to me because I believe that these few last moments in my life are going to determine my own ***placement*** in the realms of Spirit when I leave here.

So—those few last moment of my own life become very important to me.

So—in a way, spiritually speaking, I say to myself that the life I've been living up to this moment on this planet has been a <u>rehearsal for my own death.</u> I beliee that idea of ***rehearsing*** my own death daily ***before*** I really die sort of made a lot sense to me. I reasoned that ***repetition is the mother of skills.*** And, I can find some spiritually charge ***affirmations*** then, I can start repeating it 24/7 day in and day out.

The beauty of ***rehearsing*** my own final words ***prior to*** my own death will help me know exactly how I will get away from my body cleanly and where I'm going to place my own consciousness.

For me death now seems as natural as breathing and ***rehearsing*** my own death daily has become a second nature to me, a sort of a reflex that my mind is now habitually repeats my spiritually charged final words: ***Lord, I did the best I could.*** I call this for lack of proper words as ***Stalking the Spirit.***

I earnestly believe that this spiritual insight of ***rehearsing*** my death was added onto ***me*** by constantly repeating "I Let God make perfect in me what was started." By my nightly ***inner-travels in the realms of Spirit*** as a part on rehearsal for my death.

The key is to never ever stop searching until we have found it all!

I don't know what God has in store for me, but I feel so serene and at peace 24/7 that it does not matter. What do I have to be afraid of when I am one with God as He is with me.

Lately, I don't know what's to become of me. It seems that a tranquil soul and a quiet spirit come to me even while I sleep. If I'm having hard time going to sleep I repeat my death ***rehearsal*** words silently and to myself until I do go to sleep. Because I am at rest the trails of life bring me no suffering because I know: *"**this too, shall pass.***

And, it always does because it's a promise of God. I just maintain the practice of the presence of God. I know my mind is my own enemy because it will go against me in my Spirit. And it seems to win because the mind acts like a little devil sitting on my shoulder telling me how bad people and things are. One easy way for me to prevent my mind from wandering away from God is tti 'train' myself to dwell in God's presence all day long.

This provide a sort of "practice" for me, as I remind myself to concentrate on God. Remaining in God's presence 24/7 thus it becomes easier for me to do.I must admit, that my sole occupation in life is to please God no matter what I have sacrifice for it, even my own life.

I've have walked with the Lord for forty plus years. I have often wondered who, by His mercy, called me for that purpose?

As I often think of blessings God has bestowed upon

me and still continue to give me I praise Him and thank Him from the bottom of my own heart. I do know for a fact that I cannot avoid the dangers of life without God's continued help, so I ask Him for it ceaselessly. I *can* ask for His help because I'm with Him 24/7 day and night, anytime anywhere.

I will cultivate the spiritual habit of *thinking of God twenty-four hours, seven days a week and 365 days a year after year until I die.*

My personal promise to God.

Frankly, I don't know an easier method, nor do practice any other, so I advise this one to everybody. The point I am trying so hard to make is that *I have to know someone before I can truly love Him, so it makes perfect sense* (to me anyway) *that in order to know God, I must think about Him and I must practice the presence of God often.*

And once I get to know Him, I'll *think* of Him often. *I think about God as often as I can, day and night, in*

everything I say, do, and even think. ***You might say, I am
living with God and loving it.***

I believe that it would be unfair if I did not mention that my
whole family has been very supportive of my determination
to maintain the practice of presence of God 24/7.

There can be no richer person than with an understanding
spouse and family. My wife and children have given me
more than that they ever received from me, in ways that
only a father and a spouse can truly know.

CHAPTER FIVE

How I do my Meditation as Observation

One of my spiritual masters (John-Roger) often taught me something that I never forgot. He said that we do not *judge* the meditation. We do not judge the mind or the emotions.

We observe them, and the observing itself dissolves our negative emotions That is how we get free, that is how we dissolve negative karma. By doing the following seven meditations (spiritual exercises) has helped me not only to maintain the presence of God—but—taught me to be as ecstatic, as God- intoxicated as I want to be. Just think of it!

Seven Spiritual Exercises:

I believe that since you are so seriously interested in knowing how to maintain the practice of the presence of God, I will try to explain it through the seven spiritual exercises that I learned from my Spiritual teacher long ago.

In all honesty, although I found many books describing how to know God and mature spiritually, I believe they only confused my Soul. What I wanted was simply to belong totally to God not in just theory but, as daily living reality in my life.

The information that follows may seem rather abstract. It's Okay if you don't fully understand it. Just allow your inner wisdom to absorb it. Keep reflecting on the issues suggested here. You'll find your understanding of them deepening more and more as you progress.

In August of 2019, I had the opportunity to visit my family in my homeland Pakistan. One day I met a very famous artist who showed me his world famous painting about the nature, all things living and the universe and specially about the soul. I truly enjoyed looking at his outstanding paintings. I was indeed very impressed by work of art.

One of his paintings caught my attention. This artist had painted beautiful flowers, trees and people. Then, this artist told me that when his father saw this painting for the very first time, he said: ***"Flower buds are nice but be sure not to paint faces because Allah will ask you to put Soul in them".***

Suddenly, I began to ponder on what his father had said to him about Soul. I began to meditate and contemplate on **what if God had asked me to help mankind and humanity** to become *aware of our souls not, just in theory but, a living reality in human life.*

I believe from the bottom of my heart, if this book helps only a single person to Experience the *awareness* of himself or herself then my forty plus years of hard work will have been well paid.

Spiritual Exercise One

My spiritual master has taught me that I came into this world for the sole purpose of fulfilling my spiritual promised which is: **to find out who I am, and to find out where the Soul realm is in the hierarchy of the thirty-three realms of Spirit—and, to go there, and a have a co-creative** consciousness **with God.**

My daily practice of the presence of God helps me fulfill my promise. I believe this is my whole purpose on this planet earth. But, my own mind plays devil's advocate in the Spirit that is why my mind is my enemy **not** as a victim no matter what is happening.

I let the Spirit guide me with its knowledge and inner-wisdom. Sometimes it warns me ahead of time, and other times it just walks me into a situation and see how I can handle it.

Spirit makes my own everyday life magical when I try to open my 'third-eye" and activate the Pineal gland of my brain to 'experience' myself as Soul and as one with God not, just in theory but, as a living reality in my daily life.

Spiritual Exercise Two

My spiritual master says: ***"It is obvious that the Spirit*** (The Divine part within us) ***does not care if it is fair or not fair. Spirit is ruthless in the sense that if my own 'intention' isn't directed toward it, it does not reveal It- self to me.***

As I look over my own past forty plus years of search to find out "***Who I really am?*** I can really say "amen" to that and I'll tell you why? I've spent more that forty long years in my own spiritual pursuit trying to not ever reaction to the material world.

The point is that for forty plus years I have sacrificed anything and everything but, not my God-given power and the privilege to take full and complete possession of my own mind's ***thinking*** 24/7.

Spending more than forty long years of my own life in spiritual pursuits and sacrificing anything and everything to keep my inner ***intention totally 'fixed'*** only on my prime spiritual goal, is an experience, isn't calculated to give you a sustained hope, *I assure you.*

But, I knew right from the beginning that, ***if I can change my spiritual consciousness. I can move toward the convergence point.***

I can spend more of my time in spiritual pursuit instead of just reacting to the material world. I can remain in peace. I can never control God, but I can, very definitely "align" and flow with His will. That I can surely do.

(When the Spirit and soul 'merge' together the *blend* **in the middle is called Convergence).**

So—what's the point? The point I am trying to make here is, after forty plus years of trials, tribulations, and troubles that I had gone through to finally reach my destination to become ***aware*** of myself as a ***Soul***, a divine part of almighty God, ***the Spirit, didn't even say "hello" to me or do anything or gave any signs of meeting me.***

Perhaps, it is being a bit childish, but that's exactly how

my own soul felt at the moment of my encounter with (Spirit) the divine part of all mighty God. It did seem to me, anyway, at that moment, like a gross unfairness.

Perhaps, it was my own physical-self who has no clue to the spiritual-self, the **God- self** within me. ***It did, however, made me wonder that what is this "thing" inside of me that stops me from knowing "Who I am, and of recognizing my own Soul and of "experiencing" the divine, deep love of God that transcend all.***

Suddenly, I remembered what my spiritual master had taught me that: ***my own mind is my enemy*** because it will always go against me in my Spirit. And let me tell you, from my own personal experience the mind won—***big time***—for forty long years.

My mind would often challenge me to demonstrate just how much I mean in my desire for ***converging my Spirit back into alignment.*** But, worst of all mind would attempt to destroy and wreak havoc and vengeance and set loose the dogs of war (so to speak) on my spouse, or my kids, or even myself.

People, friends and associate would try to antagonize me for no reasons, baiting me to strike them. I would try my level best to withhold the strike, knowing full well that the **karma** they set in motion well be worse than any blow. My mind would do anything and everything in its power to keep me from knowing what is going on.

The sad thing is that my mind is often testing, doubting, and holding back. But, you know what? My own mind with all these tricks actually make me more determined for coming into alignment with my Spirit. Do you know why? I'll tell you why" Because, I'll bet that my mind is truly afraid that I will leave the mind behind when I do practice the presence of God 24/7. And to my amazement, that's exactly what has happened to me by the practice of the presence of God.

Spiritual Exercise Three

My spiritual master taught me: ***"When I was born in this world I left a spiritual where I existed as Spirit*** (A Divine part of God) ***as pure love, where everything was just perfect, and constantly doing the God's will in His way."***

So—when I decided to come into this physical, material world, ***I find that it does not always go as expected in the way I saw it when looked down into the material world and from the high plane of love where I saw that I could do everything in this physical world perfectly.***

My spiritual master continued:

He said:

"So—then I decided to come into this place called earth—and although everything here on earth is still indeed, perfect just the way I saw from the high plane of love—I just don't like it the way it is here on earth.

He said: ***the problem isn't what is here. The problem is in my on "attitude what is here."*** What I'm trying to convey here to you, said my spiritual master, ***"that When***

67

I existed in the Spirit world, I existed in my Spirit-body and not in the physical-body. In the physical world, you are both, the physical being and the spiritual being at the same time.

In the next ***Spiritual Exercise Four***, I'll talk about two key things.

First, I will talk more about the third-eye and how to 'activate' the Pineal Gland of the human brain to open the "third-eye".

Second, I'll share with the reader just ***who gave me the true inspiration behind the book.*** You may even know this person.

Spiritual Exercise Four

As promised, please allow me to share with you just how the ***inspiration*** for this new book came into my mind. I recall as if it was yesterday that back in October 5th 2011, there was an article on the ***internet*** about **Steve Jobs** posted on aol.com by Tom Stevens on October 5th 2011.

As some of us may remember that Steve Jobs was one of **the co-founders of Apple computers.**

Steve Jobs served as the CEO of Apple in the 1970s and '80s, and returned to the company in 1997 to serve again as CEO until 2011.This article on the internet, posted the head-lines that read:

Here is STEVE JOB himself, IN HIS OWN WORDS. The message from Steve Job under the head-line read:

"Because the people who are crazy enough to think they can change the world are the ones who do."

R.I.P. Steve Jobs.

Frankly, I almost deleted the email message on the internet on aol.com.

But, I did make hard copy to frame it and hang it in my study room. (I still have that original message from the internet). The funny this that every time I would look at Steve Job's message: *"Because the people who are crazy*

enough to think they can change the world are the ones who do." I will get "goose-bumps".

I remember that, I would say to myself—Yeah! Sure, **I'm crazy enough to believe that I can change the world.** I almost threw the hardcopy of Steve Jobs message out of the window and I tell you why?

Because I was just a foreign student from Pakistan who could not speak much English, and had very hard time getting admission in some of the reputable colleges and universities in the United States of America.

But you know what?

As God is my witness, I always felt the presence of something, or someone (non-physical) within me who through some kind of a 'miracle' (I call them the 'turning-points" in my life) guided me toward what I needed to do or where I need to go, or who I need to see at the right place and at the right time.

But, most importantly, this 'inner-wisdom gave me the

courage to just follow through with it without any opposition or rejection.

I truly became well off just following this inner wisdom that longs to communicate with me and love me. One side effect of recognizing, relating, assimilating and applying this commands of someone within me is that I began to sense as if I am seeing the world through the eyes of someone within me.

I would hold an intelligent conversation with others, make intelligent decisions and choices in my life mattes, but to me, it was as if someone else *inside* of me was doing all the talking or making all the decisions for me.

For a while, I thought that I was going crazy, but since it didn't hurt me, and made the right decisions and choices, I just remained quiet on the subject because I knew that I'll be most likely misunderstood if I mention my condition to other well meaning people including friends an relatives.

I must admit, everything wasn't just easy. I often did go through many difficulties. There is a Biblical verse that says: ***"Take courage! God often allows us to go through difficulties to purify our souls and to teach us to rely on Him more.***

Suddenly, I began to offer God all my personal, social, professional problems unceasingly, and ask God for the strength to overcome them. ***I began to talk to Him often and never forget Him even and mostly praise Him for everything. I would go to God humbly and lovingly—as dear friend.***

When the difficulties are at their worse I go to God and say: ***Lord, I can't take it any longer!*** Many times tears would start to fall from my eyes as a stream of water. Over the past forty plus years while practicing the presence of God, one thing I've found is that God ***never*** leaves me unless I go away first.

I do my level best to never ever separate myself from God's presence. It has become a reflex or a second nature for me. For me, the practice the presence of God has become a ritual which I will do for eternity. I will live with God now and die with God when my time is at hand.

To be honest with you, my daily practice of the presence of God is just a ***rehearsal for the last thing I'll do before I die and meet me Creator the very first time and humbly say: Lord, I did the very best I could do.*** I believe that that's all God asks of me.

With that in mind, let's focus on our ***Spiritual Exercise Four.***

I'll bet that you might thought that I forgot it. No way, So-lets now talk a little bit about the "third-eye". Spiritual masters of all ages who have spent a life-time in Soul travels and habitually visiting the realms of Spirit through the "third-eye" and are able to activate the Pineal gland of the brain say that "we don't really belong here on earth— ***Spiritually!*** Perhaps, that is why, we have such a hard time living here on earth.

Speaking for myself, I've often wondered that why do we have such a hard time making ourselves do what we want to do according to our intention? The reason is, that our intention only functions in the spiritual world. Just think of it!

Sure, we have advanced enormously technologically through using the mind rightly, but we are still acting like the stone age or during the ancient biblical days by using the mind wrongly. That is why the mind is our biggest enemy because it will go against the human race in all the matters of Spirit.

I remember the biblical story of the *Adam* and *Eve* (the parents of the Human race) who disobeyed the God's wishes not to ever eat the fruits of the forbidden tree in the garden of Eden.

And, I also remember the story of the Devil who also disobeyed God for not bowing before *Adam* became the birth of the reality of the 'duality' of living in the physical world which created the reality of the good and bad on the surface of the earth. So—the human mind came under the control (so to speak) of the Devil.

I believe, that under the control of the Devil the mind makes sure that human being never find out easily the spiritual worlds such as the realms of Spirit, or the *Kingdom of Heaven* or the *Kingdom of God.*

Why? Because *Adam* (the first human being) was responsible for having been thrown out of the *Kingdom of God.*

OPENING THE "THIRD-EYE".

Opening the "third-eye" is about "*seeing through the eyes of the Soul*", my Spiritual master used to say. It's about making our own life magical by spending more time in spiritual pursuits instead of reacting to the material world. And, when really know that I'll live in freedom and the fulfillment of my own spiritual promise. This can easily be made possible by opening the "third-eye".

CONNECTING HEART WITH HEAD.

The information I now share with you may seem somewhat abstract, it certainly was for me too. But, once

---

Rev. Dr. Mushtaq Jaafri

I did understand the full the significance of *Connecting Heart With Head, It hit me like the jolt of lightening.*

Suddenly it dawned on me that we use the "energy" of the heart' because our heart is the center of this gut feelings and closely 'connected' with our guidance and inner experience of ***who we are as a Soul not just in theory but and*** as one with God in our daily life.

We also use the structure in our brain called the ***pineal gland of the brain*** which is commonly known as the "third-eye"

The "third-eye is nothing more nor less than a symbolic connection we already have with the Higher-Mind or the Higher Source. or whatever you want to call it) as a Soul and s one with God.

Spiritual Exercise Five

My spiritual teacher taught me:"

There is no need for me to do what I already know how to do, or try to learn what I already know because

76

I only need to learn what I do not know—and what I do not know how to do.

The funny thing is that I spend more than forty plus long years in serious spiritual pursuits not really knowing how to open my own "third-eye" and **activate the Pineal gland of my brain.**

Perhaps, that is why I always remained one step behind my own mind in its effort to go against me in my spiritual pursuits. The fact of the matter is that I could never really overcome **the five "passions" of the mind namely: Anger, Greed, Lust, Vanity and attachment** (to material world).

No matter how hard I tried to control my own mind by controlling my thinking or how much I did "positive-thinking" or kept my own mind busily engaged with my spiritually inspired affirmations—the negative emotion of **Anger**—would find a way to overcome me.

It was as if someone inside of me that was doing all the yelling and dominating all other as the head of the house-hold. The negative emotion of **greed** somewhat less dominating than the *Anger*, but, Oh—boy, did the negative emotion of *lust* could overcome me?

What's even more interesting thing about these five passions of the mind is that it *wasn't* until I really learned the *art* and *science* of maintaining the practice of the presence of God and confess to God about it with these words: : *Lord, I'll never be able to overcome these five passions of the mind if you don't help me."*

Then, slowly but surely, it came to pass and I overcame them.

One of the main reasons, perhaps I could never overcome the negative passion of the mind, *vanity* and *attachment to the mater world is*, I never did really learn that the Spirit has two distinct aspects—*the Left side and the Right side of the Spirit.*

The Lift-sided Spirit could be considered as the "Path away from God, and Right-sided Spirit the "Path-toward God. The problem is that both, the Left- sided Spirit and the Right-sided Spirit are needed for coming into alignment with the presence of God.

The Left-sided Spirit is Dark where as the Right-sided Spirit is the **Light**.

I often visualize dark-sided Spirit as Devil's place where the mind plays Devil's advocate and only the Divine love exist in the Right-sided Spirit. My spiritual master used to say: **God is unknowable—but, I know God."**

My spiritual master said: Only through the right side can you and I and **everyone on the planet earth can go into the un-known where God is**. Alignment does not happen in the know, because in the tangible, everyday world there is no such thing as perfection. In the **left** and **right sides** of Spirit we find the *known and un-known.*

Spiritual Exercise Six

"There are going to be times when I am forced by the situations and circumstances to look more deeply at who I am and what I am about.?" He said to me that during

those moments take some time to look within myself, and see *who is in there, and become one with it.*

A TRUE STORY

A few years ago, due to my own mistake and stupidity a failure in a business venture in the Middle-East, I lost everything that was really precious to me, my home, my business and my belongings.

Down on my luck and nowhere to go to I was forced to look more deeply *inside* myself at who I am—but more importantly *what I am about?*

I recall as if it was just yesterday that I began to spent time in doing meditation, prayers, contemplations, and these spiritual exercises that I'm now sharing with you in this book then, in the hour of my own deepest meditation, contemplation and self-examination.

I discovered my Other-self, the self I don't normally see when I stand in front or mirror but rather I *assume* this non-physical personality within myself. I believe that it is necessary to always be **aware** of God's presence by talking with God throughout the day.

As I go about my daily business, I try to give **totally** to God in this **hectic** world and in my spiritual affairs. I can spend more of my time in spiritual pursuits instead of just reacting to the **hectic** world. I can remain at peace.

I know that no one can control God, but we can **align** with his will.

Through these seven spiritual exercises I have a clear intention toward my spiritual pursuit and reading uplifting material my intention, then achieve **presence of God 24/7, anywhere, anytime.**

Spiritual Exercise Seven

My spiritual master said: **"I stop fearing poverty find the wealth from the spirit inside me.** He said: **"Don't place value on the things of the world, instead place value on the things in your Spirit."**

As I go about my daily business, I try my level best to move into the realms of Spirit and the Spirit direct my motion. ***But. mostly I try to do my level best <u>not</u> to let my own ego, my thoughts and feelings move; instead I let God move me in all daily activities as if HE is my "inner-guide" to path toward God.***

It does not mean that I still occasionally do not lose my head or that I wouldn't have peace and tranquility or not coming into alignment with my Spirit. What I truly mean is that I let the presence of God 'move' me with Its wisdom and knowledge.

Sometime God tells me a little bit ahead of time, and other times, God just walks me into a satiation and circumstance see if I had the brain enough to handle for myself. I take it as test of God and try to handle as the best of my ability.

The interestingly enough, God would never test me more than I am capable of handling it easily.

The only point I am trying to convey here is that I let my God, move me.

People of the East, where I come from, spend a life-time

in spiritual pursuit and doing spiritual exercises for very long time at a time just get a short of the ***glimpse of the realms of Spirit beyond the Physical world.***

It is fact, that most major world's famous inventors, musicians, artists, engineers, mathematic genius, filmmakers, scientists, Space travel, are all known to visit these upper realms of Spirit on a regular basis for acquiring knowledge for their projects.

How do these world leaders, scientists and inventors find the un-known and un- knowable knowledge? Very simply, I believe that they somehow came across the know-how of techniques to know how to open the "third-eye" and 'activate the Pineal gland of the brain.

I believe that the human 'third-eye' located in the center of the forehead and is the center of human 'intuition', inner guidance, and all spiritual wisdom. It activates all the psychic senses beyond the five physical senses namely:

The sense of sight, the sense of sound, the sense of smell, the sense of taste and the sense of touch.

HUMAN HEART IS THE CENTER OF ALL THINGS

Human heart is the center of all human gut-feelings and intuition and is run and control by God Himself. God controls the human heart and circulation of the blood though. I've seen people in the East, who have never seen inside of a hospital because of any physical illness.

Are they super human beings?

Of course not.

They are just as human as any one of us on earth.

But, they do know something about the working of the mind and the power of God.

Speaking for myself, at the time of writing of this manuscript, I am 83 years old and every time I sense a minor 'heart-attack" coming on, I summon God and Lo and Behold all is well again. People say that they have a 'migraine head ache'

I often wonder what is it inside of me that controls everything?

Please understand, I don't tell you all this to impress you. Far from it.

I tell you all this what is possible if you maintain the presence of God in this hectic world.

Lastly, let me say this that I believe that when someone surrenders himself or herself completely to God, resolving to do anything and everything to for God, the Lord will protect him or her from any hardship physically or mentally. The sad thing is that it sounds too simplistic to do.

CHAPTER SIX

A Message from God for me!

Your task is to build a better world." Said God and I answered, *How? This world is such a large vast place, and, oh so completed now, and, I am so small and useless, there is nothing I can do.*

But, God in all His wisdom said, *You just build a better you.*

What that means in plain language is that I *MUST find* constant pleasure in God's divine company, seeking humbly and lovingly *conversation* in any way at every moment.

For me, this is especial important in time of my great sorrows, sufferings or temptations and even in times of unfaithfulness and sins. That is why *I try to converse with*

God in little ways every time, day or night 24/7. I try to reveal my heart to God as the words come to me.

People ask me, *How can I recognize God and 'experience His deep love that transcends all?* And, I always say: *the best I can."* I've now reduced my own life to just one thing that is *Seeking God 24/7 because it makes it possible for me to remain in the presence of God.*

I'll now attempt to answer the most frequently asked questions. Since the repetition is the mother of skills, you may find repetition of some of the key things discussed.

Q. If you are not your own mind, then, *who are you?*

Ans. Spiritually speaking, you are an *awareness,* <u>behind</u> the '*thinking'* of mind.

The word *'awareness'*, in way I use here is *synonymous* with the word *unknowable—so, when I say "God is unknowable—but I know God,* what I'm really saying is that *I've become aware of myself as Soul not just in theory but a 'living' reality in my daily life.*

Spiritually speaking it simply refers to "Soul Transcendence." Meaning, as Soul, I'm a divine part of *who God Is.* It allows me to converse with God and remain in the presence of God.

HERE'S THE CLUE!

The moment I can truly recognize, relate, assimilate and apply the formula that I am an awareness behind my mind's thinking, it becomes a sort of an *awakening* process which is the *Separation of mind and thinking.*

FIRST AWAKENING PROCESS IS THROUGH THE "ACT" OF "GRACE.

Many years ago, after my forty plus years of practicing the *awareness* of myself as Soul, my very first *awakening* process came into my life as an 'act' of grace. I recall as if it was just yesterday, I was sitting in the parking lot of my office building reading a motivational book the *Power of Now* and suddenly I received my own very first 'glimpse' of the *awakening* process which is the *Separation of thinking and awareness.*

It hit me like a jolt of lightening—*Wham!*

Suddenly, it dawned on me that I am in reality, an *awareness* of the *un- knowable, God, between the thinking of the mind, and my own awareness of my own mind's thinking.* The point I'm trying to convey here is that:

This 'act' of the 'grace of God, and this vivid glimpse of a my new *awakening* process, gave me a sort of the *'legitimacy'* and a proof-positive (at least to my own satisfaction) that *I am not my own mind—instead I am the observer* (awareness) *behind my own thinking mind.* I was on cloud nine (so to speak)

After forty plus years, for the very first time in my own spiritual pursuits, *I could see my spirituality through my own physical individuality.* Furthermore, perhaps for the very first time in my own life, I could verify (so to speak) that in essence, *I am a spiritual being having a physical experience* here on earth—

Perhaps, the biggest reward of this new *awakening* process in my own life as a direct result of this *un-knowable* (GOD) came that I began to spend more time in spiritual pursuits—instead of the material world.

I literally, became aware of myself as Soul (awareness) behind my 'thinking- mind' and became *totally* one with (un-knowable) God as He is one with me not in just theory but, a living reality in my daily life.

I began to remain in the presence of God 24/7.

Sure enough, this 'act' of grace began to assist me in the convergence of my own Spirit (God) back into alignment and the rest, as they say, is history. I know that this information may seem somewhat abstract. It's Okay if you don't fully understand it.

Just allow your inner wisdom to absorb it. Keep reflecting on the issues suggested here.

You will find your understanding of them deepening more and more as you progress. The position I am in is the best position for my own learning, for my growth and for my own spiritual expansion.

Q. People complain that they have been doing meditation, contemplation, and spiritual exercises to find God and all they see is darkness. They get quite irritated and very angry on my claims about my conversation with God.

Ans. I believe that it is an excellent question and deserves an honest answer.

My spiritual master always said: ***Remember, I don't have to 'do' anything with that darkness. Get-rid of my false exceptions of what spiritual experience means: just be silent and 'observe' my darkness.***

Try to realize that God is truly trying to 'speak' through the 'blackness' that I see in my forehead during my meditation, contemplation and spiritual exercises.

The problem with me is that I am so busy being 'uptight' and resenting it that I fail to ***hear*** God' voice.

My spiritual master further explained that I do not ***judge*** the meditation, contemplation or spiritual exercises, and I do not *judge the mind or the emotions,*

I just 'observe' and the darkness in the middle of your forehead, and you'll be surprise to see that my 'observing alone by 'itself *'dissolves' my own negative emotions.*

I asked my spiritual Master: *"What will be left when all my own negative emotions are dissolved?"* My spiritual Master said: *"If you ask, you are losing."* But if I can be *silent* and *observe my darkness and try to realize that God is speaking through the darkness and do not judge what is happening and then place it., that love will move the disturbance.*

That is how I get free; that is how I dissolve negative karma. Strangely enough, I began on my own spiritual journey and, totally spontaneously, something happened to lift me and brought to God.

By my daily practice to maintain the presence of God—I am now trying to share with you what that was, and *how* make that happen every time I meditate, contemplate or doing my daily spiritual exercise.

My spiritual Master taught me that: ***Do not judge what is happening and by placing deep love of God in it—I can be as deep, as ecstatic, as God-intoxicated as I want to be.*** Just think of it!

Q. *How can I bypass the Mind and free the Soul?*

Ans. I get a big kick out it, when people meeting me for the first time, *focus* upon my face, my physical body and think that it is me.

They have looked at me photograph, and when they meet me in person they are skeptical ***unless*** my face is the way it was in the photograph.

Just think what restrictions that puts on our knowing ourselves and each others. I used to ask myself: ***Are we only a physical beings and not a spiritual being?*** For forty plus long years, I really lived with this non-physical being inside of me who loved me and longed to communicate with me. I held daily conversation with this Spiritual being inside of me.

So—I often wonder why can't I see it or atleast, 'experience' the presence of God, or Spirit or Soul within me. I thought, it was pretty logical question and not a trick question.

Then, I finally found my answer from my Spiritual Master. He said: ***When you go to see the Soul, you mostly see your thoughts and nothing else. So you say, there is nothing else. If there were, I would be able to see it. Then, he said that, the reason I can't see the Soul's existence because it is "wrapped-up" in me.***

My Soul is what keeps me alive, not my mind. The mind, as strong as it may sometimes seem, is not always to be trusted. The Soul is solid ground. So—the big question is that ***how can I "bypass" the mind and free the Soul?" it's an excellent question.***

EVERY ONE HAS A DIFFERENT ANSWER

I believe, if you ask this question to one hundred people, you'll probably get one hundred answers—and all would by right—according to their own understanding of the working of the human mind.

For forty plus years, I have taken this challenge and for one way for me has been to try to become *aware* of my own 'thought' 24/7.

The moment I become *aware* of my own thinking and start to *observe* them, I notice, that all the thinking of the mind starts to subside and eventually leave the mind just like magic.

As a result my *awareness* behind my own 'thinking-mind' allows me to 'bypass' (so to speak) the mind and *free* the Soul. My spiritual Master called it— *the Soul Transcendence.* For more information log on: www. msia.org.

Q. What is the Pineal gland of the brain?

Ans. Pineal gland is a small structure in my brain, it is just there. This is my "inner-eye" *This is the "eye" that sees everything.*

This is a 'tiny' physical structure inside the head that can and does receive the Holy-Light of the Spirit and responsible for various spiritual processes in the mind— such as opening the "third-eye".

I imagine this Pineal gland in my brain as full size—just the size of my 'eye' inside my head *as a red dot, a black dot, or a purple dot.* I put my *intention* on these dots in the center of my head to help open my "third-eye"

Whatever I do, even if I am meditating or contemplating or even just doing my spiritual exercises, I *stop for a few moments—as often as possible—to praise God from the depts. of my own "heart" to enjoy there in secret.*

Since, I do believe from the bottom of my own *"heart"* that God is always with me no matter what I may be doing then ***why***, shouldn't I ***stop*** for a while to adore my loving God to petition Him, to offer Him my own ***"heart" and to thank Him 24/7.***

Somehow, I always have this feelings that God love me to always thank Him, praise Him and Love Him. Every time I say that: "I love You God—but, You know that."

Suddenly, I am lifted to a higher level of spiritual elevation. I begin to experience a sort of 'sweet', 'tiny' tingle in my own head. I suddenly, begin my conversation with God.

I really don't know just how to explain all this because I can't. I can only 'experience' it. I often tell myself that: ***"What could please God more than for me to leave the cares of the world temporarily in order to worship Him.*** And, I can do that anywhere, anytime, day or night 24/7.

The sad thing is the most people fear that if they spend more time with God and not to their wordily needs then, they would be a failure in the physical world. In the Christian

Bible it is written: "**Seek first, the Kingdom of Heaven, then, all the rest will be added onto you.**"

I really took hold of the God's promise. I was willing to sacrifice anything and everything (even my own life) to prove this God's message right. God said that: "**All the rest** (that includes the physical world) will be added on to you and me and every other on the planet earth if we seek the Kingdom of Heaven first). God still raises up men and women, who are willing to give all to God without any rewards.

In this way, I did find that I can partake of all virtues found in God. **What a precious reward for just honoring the love of God. Here's what my forty plus spiritual pursuits have taught me.**

I know this for a fact that my God is one with my Soul, and my Soul is one with God—and only practice of the presence of God demonstrate that to me. My Spiritual Master taught me that **All things are possible to me if I**

believe, hope and love and mostly practice the presence of God 24/7 anywhere, anytime.

I believe my own life here on earth is to practice the presence of God and that I will be doing for eternity. Perhaps, that is why, I daily rehearse my death by repeating my last word before my death.

My last words just before I meet my creator will be: ***"Lord, I did the best I could."*** Another my last-words before dying will be: ***My God I am all yours. Do whatever you 'will' with me."***

I believe that without this complete and full submission of my ***heart*** and mind to God's 'will' He cannot work in me to make me perfect (God-like) This makes me more dependent on the 'grace' of God.

I confess that I need His help with every little thing and at every moment, because without His help I can do nothing. My biggest problem in this world is that the ***flesh,*** and the ***devil*** wage a fierce and continuous battle on my Soul.

If I am not capable of humbly dependent on the 'grace' of God for His assistance, my Soul would be dragged down. Most recently,

My spiritual Master has taught me the union of the Soul and God. He said: "The first way in which Soul is united with God through the blessings of the ***Salvation, soley by God's grace.***

This is followed by a period in which a saved Soul comes to know God through a series of inner 'experiences' some of which bring Soul into closer union with Him

The Soul learns which activities brings God's presence nearer. Soul remains in God's presence by practicing those activities.

The most perfect union with, for me, is the actual presence of God. Although Soul's relationship with God is totally unique, dynamic, because the Soul is not asleep, but powerfully awake and excited. It is not the simple expression of the heart, like saying: "Lord, I love you with all my heart."

So—what is "actual presence of God?

You may ask:

My answer:

For me, the presence of God, which includes any and all kinds of communion I can have with God in Heaven. This **conversation occurs in the depths and center of my own Soul.**

Although meditation, contemplation and spiritual exercises were difficult at first for to **maintain**, it has marvelous effect on my Soul when it is faithfully practiced.

The most amazing part of faithfully practicing the presence of God is that it draws the 'grace' of God down in **abundance** and shows my Soul **how to see God's presence everywhere with pure and loving vision, which is the holiest, firmest, and the most effective attitude for meditation, contemplation and spiritual exercises.**

For me, the practice of the presence of God **strengthens me in hope.** My hope increases as my **faith** presents God's '*secrets*' through my daily practice of my spiritual exercises. No skill or special knowledge is needed to go to God.

All that is necessary is a heart dedicated entirely to God out of love for God— above all others. That is all!

In the next chapter, I will share a profound 'secret' that has truly helped me understand who I am and where my home is—and to find it and go there because it is my sole purpose in life here on earth.

CHAPTER SEVEN

"My Knowledge of the Creation by God"

First of all, please allow me to introduce my Spiritual Master to you—his name is **John-Roger.** He is the founder of the worldwide movement called the ***Movement of the Spiritual Inner Awareness.***

This International movement is based in Los Angeles, California USA and currently, I'm the second ***"Initiate"*** in the hierarchy of the realms of Spirit. For more information about this International movement please log on: <u>www. msia.org</u>.

In this chapter, I will give you the information that I have gained through the teachings of the ***Movement of Spiritual Inner Awareness.*** It's called MSIA for short.

My spiritual master has taught me that, when I was born in this physical world, I sacrifice a Spiritual world. In the Spiritual world in which I lived as ***Spirit*** and the divine part of the Supreme creator God.

I must have looked down into this physical world and looking from that high pure love realms of Spirit, I imagined doing everything with perfect love, because from the place I was looking from, everything looked perfect.

Everything, here on the planet earth still perfect just the way I saw it from pure love on the spiritual world above in heaven.

The whole point I am trying to convey here is that here on earth, indeed everything is still perfect just the way I saw it from the Spiritual world, the only problem is that I just don't seem to like it here in the way it is here on earth.

So—the problem isn't that the physical world isn't perfect the way I saw from the high pure love. The main problem is that I just don't like it here the way it is.

The problem is my attitude toward it—that's all. Many

times, I feel as if I don't belong here spiritually. My spiritual master often said: ***"We are engrafted into the body here on the physical world.***

THE REALMS OF SPIRIT

The information that follows may seem rather abstract. It's Okay if you don't fully understand it. Just allow your inner wisdom to absorb it. Keep reflecting on the issues suggested by my spiritual master. You'll find, just like I did, that your own understanding of them deepening more and more as you progress toward your own spiiritual progression.

This chapter is an overview of life—my life, in Spirit as I have personally experienced it. I will present the information to you and show you how a lot of interrelates.

I share it here not as something for you to just memorize it and learn only mentally but as background information that you can have just in case you are inspired to explore the realms of Spirit beyond the Physical realm—but, perhaps, more importantly, you may be inclined to practice the presence of God and experience the both worlds the physical and the spiritual world.

This, sort of an "inner-travels" can also give you the 'glimpse' of just how large and expansive your consciousness is. You can know these realms through your direct own direct experience, at which point the information will move out of the theoretical area and becomes experiential. Remind me if I'm wrong.

Frankly I spent forty plus years to prove this wrong but I could not do it. *I'm really attempting to tell you the truth about the spiritual worlds of Spirit.* My Spiritual Master used to say:

"No matter I how close I come to describing the spiritual levels, I cannot tell you how they really are because there are no words to tell. Your own knowledge of the Realms of Spirit through an 'act' of grace in your own life if you are seeking it.

Please let me emphasize again that the reason I cannot tell you the realms of Spirit are because there are no words in the English language (or any language) to describe what is going on in the spiritual world. And as my spiritual master said to me: ***Your own experience of these 'thirty-three" realms of Spirit will be the best validation you and I can have of their existence.***

With that in mind, let's look at the first six realms of Spirit. The very ***first*** realm is called the ***Physical*** realm of Spirit. This realm of spirit is relating to the human body, that which is material.

My spiritual master said: ***"it is the realm of senses, where the Soul is trapped by the mind's five passions, lust, anger, greed, vanity and attachment to the material things.***

This physical realm is of time, space, matter and the illusion of reality of seeing the physical world as a multidimensional- awareness of yourself and all things.

The ***second*** realm of Spirit is called the ***Astral*** ream of Spirit (relating to the imagination). I am told that this second realm of Spirit is the source of all psychic phenomena—on the physical world.

The *third* realm of Spirit is called the *CASUAL* realm (relating to the emotions). It is believed that in the Causal real of Spirit, all memories, karmic patterns, past records are stored just like all information is stored (for futures use) in the memory-bank of a modern computer.

The *fourth* realm of Spirit is called the *Mental* realm relating to the mind). It is said that: this realm of Spirit, is the main source of all mental teachings, philosophies, the concept of a living God an cosmic consciousness on earth.

The *fifth* realm of Spirit is call the *Etheric* realm of Spirit (paralleling the *un- consciousness)* on the physical world. *In the East the "Etheric" realm of Spirit is known* (for the lack of proper words) *as the <u>last</u> "barrier"—between the Physical and the Spiritual worlds.*

MYSTICAL TRAVELER CONSCIOUSNESS

Many Spiritual masters of the ages shave agreed without any room for doubt that that *on the "Eheric" real of Spirit a Mystical Traveler appears who takes the MSIA Initiates beyond this fifth Ethric realm of Spirit and into the first Soul realm of Spirit and another "twenty-seven positive more realm of Spirit.*

Spirit defies any physical explanation of these realms of Spirit and must be experienced to be known. There are no words; it can only be said *that they do exist and that that it is everyone's potential and heritage to know of them.*

My spiritual master taught me that: *The Soul, experience through various forms 'incarnate'* (born), *on any of these realms at various points in its journey.*

The most beautiful part of this is: said my spiritual master: that when the Soul incarnates (born) on the physical realm, *it has the unique opportunity of 'experiencing' of all of the realms of Spirit simultaneously* (that is, the physical, astral, causal, mental and the ethric).

In a little while, I will talk about how I might have been born in this Physical world. Please read my own story with an open mind because the human mind is just like an umbrella, it works best when it is open. (laugh).

MULTIDIMESATIONAL AWARENESS OF THE WORLD

The unique thing for my own Soul to be born on the Physical realm of Spirit at this particular time and space is that my own Soul's *awareness* on the Physical realm is *Multidimensional- Awareness—meaning the soul can 'simultaneously 'experience' all negative and positive realms of Spirit while in this body.* Also. this *awareness gives the legitimacy of this wold being just an illusion.*

For forty plus years I've by maintaining the presence of God, become *aware* of myself as Soul not, just in theory but, living reality in my daily life. Moreover, I've simultaneously, experience all realms of Spirit, For me, this fact alone makes, being in a physical body of great value spiritually, as I will explain below.

Coming into a Physical Existence

My Spiritual master taught me that: **The Soul comes from and has its home in the Soul realm. It takes on a physical body and comes here in the physical World to gain experience, and Earth provides many, many experiences.**

Here on the physical world, Soul has the unique opportunity to experience all the other realms of Spirit simultaneously (that is, the physical, astral, causal, mental and the Etheric), which are the negative realms of Spirit (like a negative pole of a battery), and experiencing the twenty seven positive realms of Spirit.

Many spiritual leaders believe that these realms of Spirit are the training- ground" (so to speak) for the Soul in a physical body to gain "self-realization' as well as God-Realization while still in the human body.

In order to give you a 'mental-picture' of just how the Soul moves into the physical, material existence let me tell you my own story of how I might have decided to be born here on earth in this body.

My spiritual master told me: ***"When I was born in this world, I sacrificed a spiritual world. When I was born here I entered into a 'condition' called 'sacrifice'.*** But, somehow; I did decide to be born in this world at this very time and space in the Eastern world. I was given the choice of choosing my parents

Interestingly enough, in the place I was looking from, everything looked perfect. So then, I decided to go into this place called Earth. And, as matter of scientific truth, everything on the planet Earth is perfect and my attitude toward is perfect

In the spiritual world where I existed as Spirit, as pure love, I looked down into this material world, and from that high plane of love I thought that I could do everything perfectly.

Then, I decided to go into this place called Earth in order to gain personal experience of the rich living in

this material world and become a co-creator with God in Heaven.

It seemed like to me as if I could have the cake and eat it too, I mean having an experience of the rich living on Earth and, the opportunity to be a Co-Creator here in heaven. But, the problem for achieving that goal was that I needed to come in the physical world in a ***physical*** body.

I must confess, that the more I thought of the idea of going to the Earth, the more I became excited. I believe, my parents were chosen for this task and my mother was chosen too. My mother was a very gentle school teacher, She was beautiful loving mother, kind, and very soft spoken and very spiritual person always praying.

Many time I would ask her, MOM, I need to go to school, please MOM—I need breakfast now! I really, couldn't understand, why, my mother was so kind to me more than all her other kids? She would worry about me if I was late from school or hurt playing games in school or flying kites on the roof of our home.

Mostly, I believe that my father had a very special part in my new evolution in my spiritual consciousness and being born as a human being in this particular body and at this time and space.

My father was a genius to say the least. My father believed in the **power of The KNOWLEDG.E. He used to say to me that education is the most essential part of life. Perhaps, that's why he choose to** sent me to America in order to acquire higher education and truly help me become what I am today.

Anyway—in order to make the very long story short—I did agree to be born on the *Physical realm of Spirit—so that I could experience all levels and condition and the knowledge of the Creation by God.*

Thus, the Earth experience became an important part of new evolution into the consciousness of God. As I mentioned already, that for this new evolution in my consciousness to take place, I had to be born into a physical body.

I had to be born in the physical world in a physical

body. **What that mean is that In order for me to move from the higher (positive) realms of Spiritual world in the Kingdom of Heaven, into down the lower (negative) realm of the Physical realm, I had to move down from the Kingdom of God into the lower realm of the Physical world.**

Remember too, I am being born from the higher realms of spirit namely:

Soul, Etheric, Mental, Causal, astral, and Physical. (From Heaven down to the Earth).

Soul, as a rule is both 'male' and 'female' but when I decided to be born into this physical world in this existence, I chose to come into this world at this particular time as a male.

Also, the, Soul, in itself, is both positive and negative, not in the sense it is 'good' or 'bad but, in the sense of the negative and positive polarity of the battery. It is complete in its 'energy' pattern—like the Creator God— is complete.

The division between the two sides of Spirit is so delicate, it can take years to learn to recognize, relate, assimilate and apply the subtle energies emanating from the two sides. And so many people (including myself) *deafen themselves to Spirit by addictions, physical, mental, emotional.*

Finally, let's now discuss about my coming into this physical existence.

The very first 'stage' of my existence was that as Soul, I needed to pick-up an *Etheric* body in the human consciousness for me to move down from the Soul realm of Spirit.

Remember, I'm still a divine part of Spirit (*God*)—but, not as a physical human being. I am still a spiritual-being in the first of the process of my evolution for being a physical being as yet on Earth. Next, I descended down one more (negative) realm of Spirit.

I moved down into the realms of Spirit and picked up the next lower realm of Spirit namely: *the Mental realm of Spirit—and covered my own Soul body, but remember, that still, I am not in the physical form and still in my mother's body.*

Likewise, I then, picked up the *Causal,* and the *Astral,* bodies in the same manner and then, *after*—up to nine months of stay in the body of my own mother,

I ultimately picked up my own unique physical body—all wrapped up in my own Soul—to experience the rich living on the Earth as a spiritual being having a physical experience in this physical material world.

No one can see me now because now I'm all wrapped up in my **Soul-body** here on Earth. My own Soul is still what keeps me alive, not my mind. My own mind, as strong and powerful as it sometime, is now always to be trusted. *The Soul is solid ground.*

Just one peculiar thing about my physical existence here in the physical body is that I came out into this physical world crying. I was wondering intuitively that perhaps, coming to this material wasn't all that great idea after all.

At the time of writing this manuscript, its been more than eighty years sine I came here in the physical experience in the material world. One key thing I've notice is, that *I don't belong here spiritually.*

I'm in my physical body having such a hard time making myself do what I want to do according to my intention, because my intention only functions in the Spirit.

In all honesty I used to think that the reason I came here into this physical world Is attempting to fulfill certain God-like qualities within myself. My spiritual master often mentioned that *"I am here to find out who I am, and to find our where my home in Spirit is, and to go there in consciousness and to have co- creative consciousness with Go.* For forty plus years, I've achieved it.

CHAPTER EIGHT

Connecting Heart with Head

The whole point I'm trying so hard to convey here is: ***Are we paying attention to the connection? Are we feeling the intuition? Are we focus on it?*** A lot of time we tend to be more ***focused on seeing through the physical eyes rather than through the spiritual eye.***

What I've found is that just as we need the physical eyes to see the physical world, the very same way, we do need the spiritual eye (***Third-Eye)*** to see all thirty-three spiritual worlds. (I'm talking about the realms of Spirit: about the ***physical realms: astral, causal, mental, ethris and the Soul realms of Spirit.***

Let me explain.

Ever notice that whenever, you go to see the **3-D** movies, they ask you to wear special glasses to see it?

Ever wonder why is it so?

Let me tell you why?

The reason is that by wearing these special glasses allows you to shut-off your physical eyes (so to speak) so that you can see the movie screen in front of you with the new special glasses. These new 3-D glasses are designed to let you see the movi on the screen through your "third-eye".

A NEW REVELATION FOR ME!

This helped me become more spiritually *aware*, of the fact, that when I put my *intention* focused on the idea of the intuitive part of my brain (Pineal gland)in the center of my own head, or the intuitive part of how I see things—then, I can tap into *Connecting Heart with Head* by just *feelings*—rather than by thinking or *reacting* to the **mind's** incessant, compulsive, useless, and repetitive thinking that occupies us 24/7, seven days a week, 365 days a year after year.

For the past forty plus years what I've found is that when I try to control my own 'mind-activity' and **not** suddenly re-act **negatively** of other people, spouse, friends and kids and particularly also to all negative **emotions** (Mind is both emotions and thinking), I find that I suddenly, begin to 'tap-into' ***Connecting Heart to Head—by feeling alone.***

In all honesty, that is when the idea of maintaining the presence of God flashed into my own mind. Now—after forty plus years of the practice of the presence of God—it has become a second nature for me.

It has become a reflex for me—much like a 'default' trigger or an automatic selection on the computer. I mean, the moment my own mind is silent, quiet or without any thinking—**Boom!**

My own mind, suddenly go into the 'default' mode (so to speak) and ***connects with the Source—God!***

This book is a collection of my own spiritual insights

into the heart of God— seen through my own spiritual exercises. I believe it is a **'message'** relevant not only for me but for all humanity—regardless of any personal religious beliefs—or even no beliefs.

Back in the East, from I come from, there are some people, just average people, like you and I, who spend a life-time in spiritual purists, doing daily meditation, contemplation and spiritual exercises sessions in an effort to open the 'third-eye' and 'activate' the Pineal gland of the brain in the center of the head to meet the 'heart-chakra'— and attempt to have a *'heart-energy' travel through the area of the 'third-eye' out upward the universe.*

This way, the internal becomes the external for them. Did you know that there are people in the Eastern world (Like India),, who sit on floor. With their eyes fully closed, and legs folded and hands on palms resting on lap meditating long.

I have seen these people of the East, meditate, contemplate

and doing spiritual exercises for hour-and-hours long in just one sitting at a time.

They seem in a whole lot of blissful state, apparently, in this blissful state as if **seeing** or **hearing** or **finding** *something* quite amusing or someone special. I often wondered that that just what is it that these spiritual people see or hear or find in those meditation or spiritual exercises moments inside of head that keeps them there for such a long time doing meditations.

I know that I myself have very hard time sitting doing meditation, contemplation or spiritual exercises for just 15 minutes at a time with 'thoughts' running all over in my mind. What I've found with profound interest is that **thinking often spoils everything, that evil usually begins with our thoughts.**

During my spiritual exercises I try my level best to reject *any thoughts* which distracts me from maintaining the presence of God.

For me, freeing my own mind of such *thoughts* usually

permits me a comfortable conversation with God. But, I must admit that it is not *always* easy. So— naturally, I wanted to know—***What is it that keeps these spiritual people meditating for very long hours in just one sitting daily***

My own mission and obsession had become to find out what is it or anything? What I discovered surprised me to say the least.

Amazingly, what I discovered is that these people who have spent a long time in daily meditations, somehow, learned the art and science of opening the "third-eye" through the Pineal gland of the brain, in order to withdraw the intention inside the head behind the two physical eyes and can concentrate on the ***ting dot*** there to see through the open "third-eye toward all spiritual worlds above the physical: (astral, causal, mental, etheric and the Soul) realms of Spirit.

Spiritual master of all ages, who have spent a life-time in spiritual pursuits affirm that they visualize and

imagine themselves, (not just looking at the various realms of Spirit), but imagine themselves 'traveling' in these realms of Spirit, and not just to memorize and learn only mentally but as a background information that they can have in case they run across these things in their own 'inner-travel'.

It can only give an inkling of just how vast and expansive the human consciousness is. You can know these realms through your direct experience, at which time the information moves out of the theoretical area and becomes experiential.

These spiritual master imagine themselves traveling from the physical, to the astral, to the causal, mental, etheric realms of Spirit. These are the negative realms of Spirit (like the negative pole of a battery) within the body.

In the East, it is a common believe that a Mystical Traveler consciousness appears on the *etheric realm of Spirit* and assist certain group of *initiates* into the Kingdom of Heaven and to the Kingdom of God above.

Above the etheric realm of Spirit, is the very first *positive* realm of Spirit (like the positive pole of the battery) In the East, the 'space' in between the negative and positive realms of Spirit is known (for lack of proper words) as the *"gap-of-no- realms"—or paralleling the Un-conscious.*

In the East, it is believed that to help an *initiate* of certain spiritual path—in his or her daily *Soul travels* from the negative realm (etheric) to the first positive realm (Soul) —a *mystical traveler* consciousness appears who assists and guides these *initiates* to the Soul real of Spirit.

How do I know this? You may ask?

I happen to know this for fact because that currently I am a minister and a second *initiate* of this spiritual path. This Spiritual Path is called the *Movement of Spiritual Inner Awareness.* (**MSIA**) for short.

All those who have intuitively, experienced traveling into these negative and positive realms of Spirit, and gone beyond into the higher positive realms of Spirit do agree with me that it surely does 'give' a legitimacy of both the negative (lower realms of Spirit) *and the positive* (higher realms of Spirit).

To be perfectly honest with you, I can tell you that nothing has influenced my own life than the knowledge and the knowing the Creation by God. Very few spiritual path teach these realms of Spirit. Log on: www.msia.org.

It help me understand that *God is un-knowable—but, I know God! It helped me give the legitimacy—of the Soul Transcendence—which is becoming awareness of myself as Soul—not just in theory—but a 'living' reality in my own daily life.*

It definitely helped me understand that I came into this world attempting to fulfill certain qualities within myself. Most importantly it helped me understand that I do have a prime directive and—"I am here to find out, who I am, and to find out where my home is in Spirit (Kingdom of God) *and to go there in consciousness, and to have a co-creative conscious with God.*

For me, to maintain the presence of God on the planet

Earth is in reality for what I will be doing for Eternity. And—the list goes on and on. But, you get the picture.

So—to sum up everything I am trying to cover here is that in essence, all you need to know is that the divine Creation is split into two parts: the lower and the higher planes.

The lower planes are the material realm of time, space, matter and 'energy' and the physical plane, of course, belongs here.

The higher planes are beyond time and space: the true spiritual worlds of God. I habitually, try my level best to travel into these higher spiritual planes during my meditation.

Here's how I do my spiritual exercises for Soul travel: *I visualize, or imagine or just pretend that lower planes below the Soul plane:* (Physical, astral, causal, mental, etheric) *are a "training-grounds"—for my own "Self-Realization".*

During my Soul travels, I remind myself that *I am here*

to find out who I am, to find out my own home in Spirit and to god there. I realize that there are two Kingdom of Heaven.

One is inside of my bodye and the second is the outside of my body. In my own mind I go to the Kingdom of Heaven <u>inside</u> me by traveling from the physical, astral, causal, mental and the ethric realms of Spirit.

Then, I go to *one outside of my body: from the <u>astral</u>, causal, mental, etheric and the Soul plane above the body.* (There are 27 positive realms of Spirit that I travel in my imagination until I reach the *Kingdom of God. The most beautiful thing about the Kingdom of God is that it is a "training-ground" for my God-Realization.*

My ultimate goal, of course, is to reach the Kingdom of God while still in my human body. This is a ritual (so to speak) that *I do to maintain the presence of God—and something I'll be doing for eternity.*

The funny thing is that when I do reach above the higher positive realms of Spirit, I really become aware of myself as Soul and as one with God—perhaps, that is why I say: God is unknowable—but, I know God. It is as if I've become one with God, all things living and the whole universe.

You have got to 'experience' it while you are still in this physical body. I believe that only human being are capable of observing the presence of God in all things including themselves. I believe that human beings are sacred and superior to all of God's creations on earth, just for this very reason.

Perhaps that is why I love to travel into the higher— positive realms of Spirit in my own visualization and imagination.

"I really don't have to die to inherit—the Kingdom of God—I can have it while I am still alive, right here— right now.

I often, imagine that I am a *heir* to the throne of the Kingdom of God—because I am divine part of God—and as such—I too have the essence of God within me.

People often tell me that there is no urgency in Spirit—because Spirit has Infinite patience for the Soul to come home in the Kingdom of Heaven.

One easy way for me is to practice the God's presence into my own life without any conditions or hinder or restrictions. My only job here on the planet Earth is to be ready to receive the Spirit at any time and at all times. I know this for sure that God did not put me here on Earth to be a beggar, ***nor,*** God, simply, put me here and said: ***"that's it"*** Go do it! ***God loves me.!***

But, My Spiritual master did warned me about the nature of the Spirit. He said: ***Spirit is ruthless. Not the kind of ruthlessness that it hits you on the head or cuts your arm off and lets to bleed to death, but ruthless in the sense that if your intention is not oriented toward it, it does not reveal Itself to you.***

And, if all the trials and troubles that you have gone through to reach it, it does not say 'hello' to you or do anything,--it seem like a gross unfair.

Speaking for myself, I'll say 'amen' to that because after my forty plus trails, tribulations, and troubles for finding the true meaning of this life that I had gone through to reach it, the Spirit didn't say 'hello' or something to me.

I personally thought it was indeed—unfair to me. But, I knew right from the beginning that this material world is just a 'training-ground' my Soul to experience

CHAPTER NINE

How I'm a Spiritual Being Having Physical Experience

Spiritual masters of all ages who consistently and consciously spend more of their time in spiritual pursuits instead of re-acting to the mind—always remain in peace regardless of what is happening in the material world. Someone once told me that only those who can **handle** adversities in life learn the art and science of living in peace.

They know as human beings: *we can never ever control God, but we we can most certainly 'align'—and flow—with God's will. In fact, I was so intrigued with this 'truth' that I did self-published a new book with a major self-publisher company AurtorHouse--under the title:* **Go With The Flow—A Way to Blissful Living.**

(available: www.authorhouse.com) referring to the above statement: that "you can 'align' and *flow—with God's 'will' but, you can never control God.*

As I recall, my spiritual master often talked about **Surrendering Control to God.** He said: *"Once we fully understand that we as human beings cannot control then,* **"We can surrender control to what is in control—God, and let Him continue to run the universe.**

The sad thing is: He said that, **"sometimes we sense God's 'hidden' powers, but we feel it as fear and we contract.** I say to myself: *Give me a break, there could never be anything in God—to inspire fear—fear in only a label we put on our own 'awe'—to His power. –a power we cannot possibly comprehend—and we only fear that we are losing control.*

So—I made a determined choice to do something—I became free in it.

Once I made a determined choice to maintain the

presence of God—I became free in fear. ***Not free from it—but, free in it.***

One key that is that I do have to often surrender control in order to receive whatever it is I am asking for in return of it.

My spiritual master often said: To surrender is to protect yourself from further harm or hurt. The only point I am trying to convey here is that in the final analysis we as human beings are truly a spiritual beings having a physical experience here on earth.

So—the next logical question for me is: ***"How do I go about experiencing the awareness of myself as a Soul— right here—right now at 'this-moment'***

In all honesty, I spent forty plus years trying to validate my experience as a Soul—not in just theory but a daily living reality 24/7, even days a week— 365 day a year after year—until I die and meet my Creator God—in person.

The practice of the presence of God gave me the

legitimacy of my becoming *aware* of myself as a *Spiritual Being Having a Physical experience here on Earth—right here, right now and at 'this-moment'.* Believe it! Since, I am a practical man, you will find that this is a very practical book not based on some hear says but based on my own forty plus years living this philosophy on a day-day basis.

What's more amazing about this book is that this book has *literally*—helped me live an inner-spiritual life in a constantly changing, challenging, and mostly demanding material world. *All I ask is use what works for you and let go of what does not.*

Before I close this chapter on our being a Spiritual being having a Physical experience here on Earth—Let me ask you as simple question:

Can you accept an enemy and say; "I Love You?."

In the East, I have heard many spiritual master and highly spiritual people of the EAST say: *I love you if you love me—and I love you if you kill me." This is a very powerful statement—wouldn't you agree?*

At the face value, most of us probably, don't really understand the true meaning of what it really mean in the plain language.

Buy, when I began to meditate and contemplate on these sage words, suddenly, it dawned on me that *spiritual speaking once I truly embrace the enemy (Accepting mind as an Enemy) within, it turns to help me.*

Then, I don't have stubbornness a bit, I have determination—because this transformed the moment I accepted it, and all the power that was blocking me before now becomes of ascension, of uplifting.

Here's what happens? Once I accept the enemy and once I embrace it, that enemy will transform and yield the power to me. I do believe from the bottom of my own heart that when you love and trust God, then, the *awakening process: The separation of thinking of the mind and your awareness of the mind's thinking to be an easy skill to master.*

For me, all it takes is to *observe* the 'mind-activity' 24/7 anytime and anywhere.

For forty plus years, OBSERVATION has been the only key thing to letting go— and let God.

I believe that human race is shifting in consciousness now where we are now ready and willing to accept the concepts as outlined in this book Not just theory base on some speculations but, based on my own forty plus years living every word in the classic book. Only me— or anyone—can discover the presence of God is through direct experience—by the practice the presence of God.

Author's Notes

This book is a reflection on my own forty plus years of spiritual understanding of the subject under discussion. It isn't intended to speak for any other modern-day religion or a spiritual path. Please understand, that I am in no way more gifted, more special or more spiritual person than you.

For forty plus years, I have been on my own spiritual path (like you), and have worked under several Eastern as well as Western Spiritual masters Just so you know—that in this book I have occasionally used terms that mean different things to different people, depending upon either the religious upbringing, or the personal path they have chosen.

As I began to practice the presence of God—and did

my meditation, contemplation and Spiritual Exercises daily, all this began to gradually become familiar and second nature to me. As a minister of the *Movement of Spiritual Inner Awareness, this delineates for me the divine line of authority by which I call forward God's Light to do work in this world.*

This divine line of authority, allows me to go forward into the world, ministering to all—regardless of race, color, creed, situation, circumstances or environment. And, at this time Spirit places a blessing. I say—hallelujah.

Printed in the United States
By Bookmasters